Religious Freedom: Why Now?
Defending an Embattled Human Right

The Witherspoon Institute Task Force
on International Religious Freedom

Timothy Samuel Shah, *principal author*
Matthew J. Franck, *editor-in-chief*
Thomas F. Farr, *chairman of the Task Force*

THE WITHERSPOON INSTITUTE

Princeton, New Jersey

Cover design by Barbara E. Williams
Book design and layout by Margaret Trejo
Printing by Thomson-Shore, Inc.

Published in the United States by the Witherspoon Institute
16 Stockton Street, Princeton, New Jersey 08540

Library of Congress Control Number: 2012931788

ISBN 978-0-9814911-9-6 (softback)
ISBN 978-0-9851087-0-0 (ebook)

Printed in the United States of America

Contents

Religious Freedom: Why Now?
Defending an Embattled Human Right

Religious freedom is under sustained pressure today around the world. In some places, it is fair to say that religious freedom is under siege. This book is a response to that sobering fact. Although scant attention is paid by governments, the academy, or the media, the implications of this crisis—and we contend that it is a crisis—are quite serious. A worldwide erosion of religious freedom is causing large-scale human suffering, grave injustice, and significant threats to international peace and security.

Outside the West, tens of millions of human beings are subject to violent persecution because of their religious beliefs, or those of their tormentors. Scores of millions more are subject to serious restrictions on their religious freedom.

In the West itself, including the United States, religious freedom is also under various pressures. Where intellectual and political leaders treat religious freedom with skepticism or indifference, it is not surprising to find encroaching threats to the conscience rights and the public witness of religious persons, communities, and institutions—and a failure to perceive the high importance of religious freedom in our relations with the rest of the world.

For the last three years, the Witherspoon Institute's Task Force on International Religious Freedom has examined the various dimensions of the challenge faced by religious freedom, and has deliberated on the most effective policy responses that can be undertaken by the United States government, and by other governments around the world. In May 2011, the Witherspoon Institute convened an unprecedented interdisciplinary meeting in Princeton, New Jersey, of more than thirty experts on the subject, from the fields of psychology, sociology, law, philosophy, theology, political science, and international relations. They included academics, policy analysts, and journalists, as well as advocates and adherents from a variety of religious traditions. The result was a focused discussion over two days of the basis of religious freedom, its present condition, and the prospects for its future.

This monograph is the Task Force's considered statement on these matters. Drafted by Timothy Samuel Shah, with contributions from Task Force chairman

Thomas F. Farr, the Witherspoon Institute's Matthew J. Franck, and the members of the Task Force, it is informed by insights from all these academic disciplines and religious traditions.

In the pages that follow, the reader will encounter the following arguments:

- Religion is the effort of individuals and communities to understand, to express, and to seek harmony with a transcendent reality of such importance that they feel compelled to organize their lives around their understanding of it, to be guided by it in their moral conduct, and to communicate their devotion to others.

- The evidence of recent anthropological and psychological research suggests that the capacity for religious belief is natural; that belief appears early and easily in the lives of individuals; that it appeared full-blown at the dawn of human civilization; and that the suppression of religious belief, expression, and practice therefore runs against the grain of human nature and experience.

- Religious freedom "in full," as we call it below, has a variety of interlocking dimensions: intellectual and spiritual; personal, moral, and practical; expressive and social; and legal and political. While no religious persons or communities have a legitimate claim to *absolute* freedom from responsibility to the polities in which they find themselves, all human beings have a right not to be coerced into abandoning their own religious convictions or adopting those of others.

- Freedom of religious faith and practice is a vital part of a "bundle" of freedoms and other social, economic, and political goods that together undergird and enable free, just, and stable societies. The protection of religious liberty is significantly and positively correlated with freedom of speech and press, civil liberties more generally, the equality of women, and economic freedom.

- Religious freedom contributes to stable political order, to social peace and the reduction of violence, and to the endurance of democratic institutions. While the introduction of protections for religious freedom, where they had not previously existed, can be "destabilizing" in the short run, there are reliable payoffs for freedom *and order* in the long run. By contrast, the repression of religious freedom is virtually certain to produce political instability, to stunt the growth of healthy civil society, and to cripple democratic development.

- Religious freedom is not merely the legacy of a particular culture or cultures, Western or otherwise. It is, rather, a universal principle of justice regarding the human experience as such. Religious freedom is essential to human dignity and integrity, a reflection of every human being's duty to form his conscience rightly, in accordance with his best judgment about ultimate truths. For each of us, it is essential to our ability to live justly—to do justice to the truth, to ourselves, to other human beings, and to our communities.

- The freedom of religion has both private and public dimensions. It is the freedom to pray, to worship, to commune with one's fellows of like mind and heart in the private practices of faith. But it is also the freedom to bear witness to one's beliefs and commitments, to be visibly religious in public life, to associate freely on the basis of religion and peacefully to encounter others with differing views on a basis of equality. It is the freedom to organize and act politically, to vote, to make arguments about public policy, and to legislate, on the basis of one's religious beliefs, consistent with principles of universal justice toward others.

- Religious freedom is not merely the counsel of secular reason. Some who hold this view argue as though the right to believe in and to act on religious principles only finds support from a vantage point independent of religion, or even thoroughly skeptical of it. To the contrary, we contend that religion can and does supply its own ground for the *freedom of* religion. It is a principle close to the heart of many religious traditions that belief and practice are not authentic if they are not freely undertaken by free persons.

- In particular, we argue that the three great Abrahamic traditions—Judaism, Christianity, and Islam—contain the internal resources to make the case for the religious freedom of all human beings to attach themselves to any faith or none at all. Preeminent scholars in all three traditions contribute brief statements, in the pages below, making a Jewish case, a Christian case, and a Muslim case for religious freedom.

- The centrality of religious belief and practice in the common experience of human beings throughout history, and the justice of the case for religious freedom, account for the prominent place given to religious freedom in legal traditions, statutes, constitutions, and international covenants in modern times. It is the hallmark of free constitutional democracy in particular to make religious freedom the "first freedom" in importance. Hence its singular place in the American constitutional tradition. Hence also its importance as a vital principle in international law, as witnessed in the Universal Declaration of Human Rights (1948) and various covenants. It is the patrimony of the leading democracies in the world, and the aspiration of peoples in developing nations.

- Nonetheless the establishment of a place for religious freedom in legal codes, constitutions, and treaties is a mere "parchment barrier" to oppression. Civil society itself, as well as governments and international organizations, must take an active interest in the defense and advancement of this universal human right. No nations, no peoples, can take religious freedom for granted as permanently secure on the basis of stated legal principles alone.

- America, the West, and the world at large have a vested interest in the advancement of religious freedom as a universal norm in all nations. Religious freedom is just in itself, and productive of other goods: peace and order; stable international relations and the defeat of terrorism and extremism; democratic development and the goods of equal citizenship. Leadership in international relations that recognizes these principles is the beginning of wisdom.

- The challenge of advancing religious freedom internationally is vitally important for two other reasons. The first is the resurgence of religion worldwide in recent years, putting paid to the "secularization thesis," the once widely held view that religious belief and practice would wane with the rise of modernity. The second is the widespread experience of the suppression of religious freedom, by governments both secular and theocratic. Hundreds of millions of human beings are, to one extent or another, the victims of such repression.

- Those two facts—of resurgent religion and of pervasive repression—are closely connected in the world's experience of religious conflict, violence, and terrorism in recent years. Islamist terrorism in particular, of paramount concern in contemporary international affairs, is the product of radical religious ideology that has incubated in fundamentally unfree societies in the Muslim world. Where religious freedom takes root, on the other hand, democracy finds support and the ideologies of terrorism are undermined.

- Deliberate steps in the formation and execution of foreign policy, therefore, should be undertaken in pursuit of global religious freedom. In the United States, recognition of religious freedom's strategic centrality came in the enactment of the 1998 International Religious Freedom Act. In the pages below, we make specific recommendations to American policymakers, to leaders of other nations and of international organizations, and to civil societies regarding the intentional and vigorous pursuit of religious freedom as a universal principle of justice, to be honored in all nations and in all dealings among nations.

Religious freedom is a large subject, and this is a small book. But our effort herein is to distill to their essence, and yet still do some justice to, the arguments sketched in the points above. **Part One**, comprised of five brief chapters on "The Ground of Religious Freedom," draws on sources as old as faith and philosophy themselves and as new as the latest findings in psychology, sociology, and political science. **Part Two**, containing two chapters on "Religious Freedom and International Affairs," turns directly to the practical strategic and political problems confronting policymakers who seek to protect and advance the freedom of religious belief and practice. Readers who are confident that they know why they are "for religious freedom" may turn immediately to Part Two and profit from it alone. But the overall argument of the book is one integral whole, and they may—we hope they will!—find themselves drawn back to Part One's exploration of the reasons for regarding religious liberty as the foremost human freedom.

We also hope that our readers will come to believe, as do the contributors to this extended essay, that attacks on religious liberty constitute a substantial and serious assault on human personhood, political communities, social goods, and global security. We hope they will join us in saying that to defend religious freedom is to advance the twin causes of human dignity and international peace.

Men and women in a great many countries are struggling to replace tyranny with stable self-government. Religious freedom is a linchpin of the freedoms that limit the powers of the state, plant firm roots for democracy, and enable it to last. It is in our vital national interest to encourage the embrace of religious liberty, as part and parcel of rejecting and, ultimately, defeating the scourges of religious extremism and terrorism. It is emphatically in the interest of movements— especially religiously grounded ones—that are attempting to break free of their nations' authoritarian histories, to see that their own future success turns upon their willingness to recognize the universal claim of all human beings to religious freedom.

It also behooves Americans, and citizens of other nations with a history of honoring religious freedom, not to become complacent about its preservation in our own midst. We are, alas, more than capable of generating our own forms of repression of the universal right to believe, practice, and witness to religious faith freely. While we look outward to the fate of freedom in the world, we must also be mindful of looking inward, and keeping our own house in order. We owe it to ourselves, to our ancestors who worked so hard to provide us with this inheritance, and to a posterity that deserves that inheritance intact. Vigilance on behalf of religious liberty, at home where our duty is nearest and abroad wherever we can encourage it, is a just response to what is highest and noblest in human experience— mankind's relation to something higher and nobler than itself.

Introduction

Let us begin with five stories. The first, depicted on the cover of this essay, occurred in the seventeenth century. The last four are happening today . . . all over the world.

Boston Commons, 1660: In 1656, the Puritans of Massachusetts Bay passed a series of laws expelling a sect of their fellow Christians known as Quakers from the colony. Should a male Quaker return to the colony, he would "for the first offense have one of his ears cut off." For a second, he would "have his other ear cut off." A Quaker woman would be whipped for either offense, but for a third, both men and women "would have their tongues bored through with a hot iron." A fourth offense warranted death. Mary Dyer, a Quaker woman, persisted. On June 1, 1660, following her fourth arrest, she was hanged on Boston Commons.[1]

Afghanistan, 2008: "An Afghan court in northern Afghanistan sentenced a [23-year-old Muslim] journalism student to death for blasphemy for distributing an article from the Internet that was considered an insult to the Prophet Muhammad." The student's name was Sayed Parwiz Kambakhsh.[2]

New Hampshire, 2009: In July 2009, in a case involving the divorced parents of 11-year-old Amanda Kurowski, Judge Lucinda V. Sadler of the Family Division of New Hampshire's Judicial Court for Belknap County concluded that the girl's "vigorous defense of her religious beliefs . . . suggests strongly that she has not had the opportunity to seriously consider any other point of view." Judge Sadler ordered Amanda to be enrolled in a secular public school instead of being home-schooled under the direction of her devoutly religious mother, Brenda Voydatch. On March 16, 2011, the New Hampshire Supreme Court upheld the lower court order.[3]

Eritrea, 2010: "Released [Christian] religious prisoners reported confinement in . . . metal shipping containers subject to extreme temperature fluctuations, . . .

[or] in underground unventilated cement cells without sanitation facilities with up to 200 other prisoners. . . . Some prisoners were hung from trees in painful positions for several weeks until they could no longer move their arms and legs, requiring other prisoners to feed and bathe them. Religious prisoners also reported being forced to walk barefoot on sharp rocks and thorns for one hour per day, beaten with hard plastic and metal rods in order to extract confessions, and threatened with death if they did not recant their faith."[4]

Egypt, 2011: "Egypt's National Council for Human Rights announced its report on the events of October 9, where 27 Coptic Christian protesters were killed and hundreds more injured outside the State TV building. . . . The report said that "anonymous" elements shot at the protesters. . . . However, the council confirmed that 17 deaths were a result of armored army vehicles running over protesters. The report said that the protesters were peaceful, only carrying wooden and plastic crosses."[5]

• • •

According to the 1948 Universal Declaration of Human Rights, adopted by the United Nations General Assembly by a vote of forty-eight to zero, "Everyone has the right to freedom of thought, conscience and religion; this right includes freedom to change his religion or belief, and freedom, either alone or in community with others and in public or private, to manifest his religion or belief in teaching, practice, worship and observance" (Article 18).[6]

At the outset of its life as the world's most representative body, the United Nations singled out a particular kind of freedom for special notice and protection—"the freedom of thought, conscience and religion." It declared that this freedom rightfully belongs to all people everywhere, not as a grant of any government or conferral by any human institution, but as a birthright. The UN was not summoning an abstract ideal. It was affirming a clear set of principles with concrete implications.

If these principles mean anything, they mean that all women and men like Mary Dyer, who believe they have found religious truth, may peacefully manifest that truth without fear of death.

The principles mean that men and women from majority religious communities, such as Afghanistan's Sayed Parwiz Kambakhsh, have the right to criticize their own faith, and that of others, without fear of prosecution, or execution, as criminals.

They mean that parents like Brenda Voydatch have the right to raise their children in their faith without fearing that the state will disapprove and force their children into secular schools.

They mean that Eritrean Christians, like all human beings everywhere, have the right to embrace the religious convictions to which their consciences lead them without fear that they will be tortured until they abjure those beliefs.

They mean that Egypt's Coptic minority, and minorities everywhere, have the right to assemble, and peacefully to seek redress of their grievances without fear of violence by government forces or private actors.

If these principles mean anything, they mean that both minority and majority religious communities have the right, alone or with others, to employ their faith in attempting to influence the public policies and practices of their nations, bringing to bear their conceptions of justice, freedom, equality, and the common good.

• • •

This essay addresses two questions:

First, is the Universal Declaration of Human Rights correct in declaring that every person possesses a right to religious freedom?
There are good reasons for affirming and protecting the right to religious freedom for all persons, everywhere, whether or not we agree with their beliefs and practices.

The Universal Declaration's affirmations concerning religious freedom are intrinsically bound up with the Declaration's foundational principles, articulated in the Preamble and first few articles. These principles include "the *inherent dignity*" and "equal and *inalienable rights of all members* of the human family" as "the foundation of freedom, justice and peace in the world" (Preamble). They include the aspiration for "a world in which human beings shall enjoy *freedom of speech and belief* and freedom from fear and want." They include the affirmation that all human beings "are endowed with *reason and conscience*" (Article 1), and all are "entitled to all the rights and freedoms set forth in this Declaration, without distinction of any kind, such as race, colour, sex, language, [or] *religion*" (Article 2).

In short, we argue that the right of religious freedom is intrinsic to the human person, necessary for human flourishing, and good for societies and their political orders.

The second question this essay addresses is: Why should we care—right now—about religious freedom? Are there reasons to treat it as a matter of urgency, not just for those who are persecuted, but for the sake of ordered liberty, prosperity, and international security?
Perhaps it is true that all the world's people should have the right to religious freedom. Perhaps it is true that some suffer unjustly. But many people suffer injustice around the world for many reasons. Are there reasons why the world's governments, institutions, and peoples should focus on religious liberty as a particular problem? Should religious freedom be an urgent policy priority, both for humanitarian and strategic reasons?

What about the United States in particular? Are there reasons that the American government and its people should care about the religious freedom of millions of others around the world? Should the United States pay special and renewed attention to the religious freedom of its own citizens?

The United States has a distinctive relationship with the matter of religious liberty. In its own constitution, law, and political self-understanding, America has been a pacesetter in institutionalizing religious freedom. Its commitment to the free exercise of religion can be understood as a continuing attempt to right the wrong done to Mary Dyer and others like her, and to invite her, and her ideas, into the life of the republic. In part because of this history, the U.S. formally incorporated a commitment to religious freedom abroad in its foreign policy through the 1998 International Religious Freedom Act (IRFA).

And yet, despite this tradition, some Americans openly suggest that religious freedom does not deserve urgent or special attention in American law or foreign policy.

Some suggest that singling out religion and religious freedom for special protection is inappropriate and perhaps even unconstitutional. Others suggest that religion deserves no more special toleration or political protection than other "deep commitments," such as other convictions of conscience, or philosophical commitments. Some say that more and more "secular" people who have no religious affiliation populate American society, and that such people should not have fewer freedoms and privileges—including exemptions from otherwise generally applicable laws—than religious people. Some judges appear to believe that too much religion is not good for children, and that it is the government's job to compel secular remedies.

Still others argue that American foreign policy faces too many urgent threats and challenges, and America's economic resources are too scarce, to permit the U.S. to focus much attention on "humanitarian" issues such as human rights and religious freedom. Even if it is true that religious liberty is an important right that all people have, America has too many other problems to make the advancement of that right an urgent priority.

• • •

This essay avows that we have many good reasons for concluding that religious freedom deserves special notice and urgent protection. Religious liberty is a universal imperative of basic justice. It is not a social luxury. It is not a matter of political charity. It is just as the Universal Declaration frames it—a matter of fundamental human rights.

This essay also argues that there are many good reasons for regarding religious freedom as a matter of great importance and urgency. We should care very much whether the religious freedom of people around the world is secure and respected, or whether it is subject to widespread diminution and systematic attack.

To preview some of the ideas that will be elaborated in the course of this essay: the answer to the first question is straightforward. There is a simple, powerful argument that religious freedom represents a universal demand of justice.

Human dignity.

The personhood, dignity, and worth of every person deserve our respect. Consider the American Quaker Mary Dyer, the Eritrean prisoners, the Muslim journalist, the Egyptian Copts, or the American mother. Their embrace of religious beliefs and practices—so evidently central to their respective identities, well-being, and sense of purpose and value—should have made them all immune from physical attack, manipulation, or impediment. Of course, there may be prudential reasons for limiting religious freedom. When religious practices violate the fundamental rights of others, civil authorities have a responsibility to intervene. As the UNDHR puts it, restrictions on religious liberty are warranted when, and only when, "necessary to protect public safety, order, health, or morals or the fundamental rights and freedoms of others."

But the beliefs and practices described above did not restrict the fundamental rights of others, public safety or order. Not remotely. The beliefs and practices of the people in our five stories *respected* the proper dignity and worth of the rights of others and of society. Thus their own beliefs and practices were and are entitled to be treated as products of human freedom, reason, and conscience. These people— every one of them—possess an inherent dignity and worth so profound that they cannot be bestowed or taken away by any human agency.

· · ·

While human dignity is the core argument for a universal right of religious freedom, this essay explores a wide range of other reasons to think that religious freedom is a universal right of great urgency and importance. One basic reason lies in the simple empirical fact that attacks on religious freedom are widespread, cruel, and consequential in social, political, economic, intellectual, and religious terms.

In fact, there are many millions of people who are subject to severe and systematic restrictions.

According to the Pew Global Attitudes Survey, in most parts of the world about 80% of people report that religion is "very important" to their lives. Yet tens of millions of people face severe political and legal pressures when it comes to their religious belief and practice. In 2009 the nonpartisan Pew Research Center reported "that 64 nations—*about one-third of the countries in the world*—have high or very high restrictions on religion." The report went on to note that "because some of the most restrictive countries are very populous, *nearly 70 percent of the world's 6.8 billion* people live in countries with high restrictions on religion."[7]

Note that word "high." The report does not find that the vast majority of the world's population faces "some" or "moderate" restrictions on religious belief and practice. It finds that most of humanity lives in countries in which religious restrictions—whether imposed by government or social groups—reach high levels of severity.

While religious minorities often bear the brunt of these restrictions, most countries with high restrictions on religion also impose significant controls on members of the majority religion. In Afghanistan, for example, Sunni Muslim reformers cannot publicly argue that the Qur'an supports the equality of men and women without risking charges of blasphemy. In Muslim-majority Jordan, all mosques are controlled by the government, regardless of whether they are publicly or privately funded, and all imams are civil servants employed and paid by the state. The result, according to one expert, is that "[t]here is no 'independent' or 'free' space in Jordanian mosques."[8]

Everywhere, millions of people do not enjoy the freedom to embrace and express those religious beliefs that conform to their own deepest convictions and judgments of conscience. Instead, they are compelled to conform their consciences and religious lives to the powers that be, whether repressive states or oppressive religious authorities.

Part One presents an argument, in five chapters, that attacks on religious freedom constitute unjustifiable assaults on human persons and their communities. Each chapter provides a case for protecting religious freedom, and each builds on what precedes it, in the order below:

(1) *The anthropological case:* What do we know about the essential human experience of encountering the divine or transcendent?

(2) *The political case:* How does that experience manifest itself in political societies, with consequences for the stability, security, freedom, and prosperity of those societies?

(3) *The moral case:* Whatever its effects, is there a case for religious freedom as good in itself, morally? What moral demands generated by human personhood and dignity are relevant here?

(4) *The religious case:* What perspective does religion itself take of the question of freedom of religion—particularly in the Jewish, Christian, and Muslim traditions?

(5) *The legal case:* If religious freedom is worth protecting, can this be done effectively through the law? What principles and doctrines characterize the American and international law of religious freedom? Are legal protections sufficient to secure religious freedom?

Part Two makes the strategic case for religious freedom. It contends that religious freedom should be advanced internationally by all nations as a means of advancing peace, security, and ordered liberty. It follows these arguments with specific policy recommendations for the conduct of the foreign affairs of the United States—recommendations that can be adapted by other nations.

Taken together, the arguments in Part Two conclude that the widespread global attacks on religious freedom constitute an assault so serious that the United States and the community of nations must consider religious freedom an issue of special policy importance and urgency.

Some evils are such an affront to human dignity and a threat to global security that they cannot be decently—or safely—ignored. Among such evils is the global assault on religious freedom.

We should be willing to safeguard religious freedom for the sake of the millions of often vulnerable people who are seeking to live out their religious convictions. If their fate is not sufficient reason, we should at least be willing to safeguard religious freedom for our own sake—and for the sake of a stable and sustainable international order.

Let us begin at the beginning. The question *What is religion?* will serve as an entry point into the anthropological case for religious freedom.

PART ONE

The Ground of Religious Freedom

CHAPTER ONE

What Is Religion?
The Anthropological Basis of Religious Freedom

We know, and it is our pride to know, that man is by his constitution a religious animal; that atheism is against, not only our reason, but our instincts; and that it cannot prevail long.

—EDMUND BURKE, REFLECTIONS ON THE
REVOLUTION IN FRANCE (1790)

Defining Religion

What kind of freedom is religious freedom? Freedom to do what? Freedom in relation to what? Before we answer these questions, we must know what religion is.

Political scientists Monica Duffy Toft, Daniel Philpott, and Timothy Samuel Shah summarize one philosopher's account of religion as having the following elements:

> (1) a belief in a supernatural being (or beings); (2) prayers or communication with that or those beings; (3) transcendent realities, including "heaven," "paradise," or "enlightenment"; (4) a distinction between the sacred and the profane and between ritual acts and sacred objects; (5) a view that explains both the world as a whole and humanity's proper relation to it; (6) a code of conduct in line with that worldview; and (7) a temporal community bound by its adherence to these elements. Though not every religion includes all of these elements, all religions include most of them, such that we understand that religion involves a combination of beliefs, behavior, and belonging in a community.[9]

Religion thus possesses several crucial characteristics. First, it concerns some kind of ultimate reality that, in sociologist Christian Smith's words, is "not normally observable with the five human senses."[10] Not all religions conceive of an ultimate reality (or what William James called the "unseen order") as "transcendent." While the "transcendent" seems to be above or distinct from the empirical order accessed by our senses, some religions such as Hinduism conceive of it as immanent rather than transcendent, as part of the empirical and hidden within it. Yet all religion characteristically concerns an unseen order, however it is understood.

Second, religion views this order as enormously significant for our lives. "[R]eligion is not simply a set of theoretical beliefs about reality," according to philosopher Joseph Boyle, "but is . . . a human response to what is ultimate in reality."[11] Included in the understanding of religion is the belief that harmoniously adjusting ourselves to ultimate reality is a distinctive good and perhaps even our supreme good.

Third, religion holds that human beings can grasp and relate to the transcendent order of reality in some fashion. Many religions also hold that at least some aspects of the transcendent order can be grasped by human reason unaided by special revelation. Many hold that the transcendent order invites and cooperates with the human striving to grasp and achieve harmony with it, and even reveals itself to human beings in some deliberate and special way. Thus religion characteristically presupposes that any distance between human beings and the transcendent order of the universe is not an unbridgeable chasm. It is not only desirable but possible to achieve some understanding of, and harmony with, ultimate reality.

Fourth, religion is something people *do* in common—a set of beliefs and practices of a community, not of isolated individuals. As Martin Riesebrodt has written, "[r]eligious actions are those whose meaning is defined by their reference to personal or impersonal superhuman powers," and these actions manifest themselves in "a complex of religious practices" that occur "in the context of an institutionalized social and cultural meaning."[12]

While religion is diverse and variable, it has been pervasive in human history and is pervasive today. If anyone has any doubts on this score, particularly those who might believe that the world is inexorably secularizing in the face of modernity, we offer numerous reasons to believe otherwise in the strategic case for religious freedom (Part Two). In most parts of the world, religious belief and practice appear to be very robust. Belief in a transcendent order of reality is, in short, quite widespread.

Religion is, in sum, the effort to achieve a harmony with whatever transcendent order of reality there may be. Religion, therefore, can be an intelligible good or aspect of human flourishing even to those who may not be "religious" in the conventional sense of belonging to an organized religion or traditional religious group. Everyone has an interest in religion, for the simple reason that no one can reasonably be indifferent to whether there is a transcendent order of reality and meaning, and to achieving whatever harmony can be achieved with such an order. And if everyone has an interest in religion, then everyone has an interest in religious freedom.

Religion's Naturalness

It is not merely a contingent fact about human history that most people have had religious experiences and have placed the quest for harmony with an unseen order at the center of their lives. From the evidence of the modern cognitive sciences, a religious disposition appears to be an essential part of human nature, as ordinary or natural to human beings as language or song. As psychologist Justin Barrett has written, "because of the nature of human minds, religious expression in beliefs and practices is nearly inevitable in most people."[13]

The cover of the June 2011 issue of *National Geographic*, with the headline "The Birth of Religion," featured a photograph of stone remnants of what is believed to be the world's oldest temple. Dating back nearly 12,000 years, to 9600 B.C.E., the sacred site was constructed in what is now Turkey some 7,000 years before the great pyramids of Egypt. "We used to think agriculture gave rise to cities and later to writing, art, and religion," the cover story began. "Now the world's oldest temple suggests the urge to worship sparked civilization." The story continued:

> At the time of Göbekli Tepe's construction much of the human race lived in small nomadic bands that survived by foraging for plants and hunting wild animals. . . . The pilgrims who came to Göbekli Tepe lived in a world without writing, metal, or pottery; to those approaching the temple from below, its pillars must have loomed overhead like rigid giants, the animals on the stones shivering in the firelight—emissaries from a spiritual world that the human mind may have only begun to envision.[14]

The people who made Göbekli Tepe may have lacked writing, metal, and pottery. But they had religion. Indeed, religion seems to have been almost the first thing they wanted. From the evidence at Göbekli Tepe, archaeologists conclude that the temple site anchored the subsequent construction of settlements and more systematic agricultural production. The city did not produce the temple, it seems, but "[t]he temple begat the city."

Religion is not only buried deep in our history, as Göbekli Tepe suggests. It is also buried deep in our psychology. Numerous cognitive scientists now hold that the impulse to seek an unseen order—and particularly a transcendent or divine agency—is deeply rooted in our nature as human beings. A new scholarly subdiscipline, the cognitive science of religion, has produced such works as Justin Barrett's *Why Would Anyone Believe in God*, Jesse Bering's *The Belief Instinct*, and Robert

McCauley's *Why Religion Is Natural and Science Isn't*. All expound the thesis that human beings are naturally religious.

In what sense is religion "natural"? The cognitive science of religion does not argue that religion is natural in the sense that it is biologically determined. According to Barrett, religion is natural "in the sense that it is cognitively easy, fluent, and automatic for people (barring developmental or environmental abnormalities), and is so because it is readily derived from the ordinary operations [of their] human cognitive equipment." Specifically, religion belongs to a set of human cognitive capacities that seem to be part of the natural maturing process. These cognitive capacities have several distinctive features. As Barrett summarizes it, "maturational naturalness seems to just appear as a matter of developmental course—as in learning to walk or talk or add small numbers." Such capacities "are broadly present across cultures in largely similar forms."[15]

These natural capacities typically arise as a matter of course in the maturation of young children—usually in the first five years of life. Some arise more naturally and easily and some require greater effort and cultural investment. Religion appears to develop easily in children. It is perhaps akin to sport, literacy, or music, in that it typically appears early in life. Religious expression does not require special cultural paraphernalia to develop. It does not take extensive training or rehearsal in order to manifest itself. By these criteria, religion appears to be very natural indeed.

As Barrett notes (in *Why Would Anyone Believe in God?*),[16] our encounter with the observable world regularly triggers a "hypersensitive agency detection device." That is, we sense things in the world that cause us naturally to discern the presence of an agent, a being capable of initiating action and thus being the cause of some effect. Voluntary agents, undertaking actions out of a conscious will, "by design" as it were, prompt us to try to make sense of the agent's mental state—his or her or its beliefs, desires, or intentions.

In sum—for reasons similar to those that undergird our belief in, and (imperfect) understanding of, other persons' minds—we find it quite natural to believe in God or gods as a kind of being who is responsible for effects we can perceive. We are also quite ready to believe as well in gods who are unseen, super-powerful, even all-knowing and immortal. The inference to a single God who is creator and cause of all is not the least surprising, given the normal make-up of our minds. Thus monotheism is quite natural, although polytheism also occurs quite naturally. On the other hand, Barrett observes that atheism is a far more "difficult" belief to attain. It requires a kind of educated *determination* to disbelieve.

The conclusions of cognitive psychologists that religion is "natural," however, can tell us nothing about whether it, or any particular manifestation of it, is rational in the sense of being fully in accord with all our reasoning about how the world works. The cognitive science of religion, that is, cannot tell us that religion is *true*, that we are right to believe in the unseen presence of one or more divine agents called gods. Much less can it tell us *what* religion, if any, is true. These are the questions of philosophy, of metaphysics and theology.

Some cognitive scientists erroneously conclude, on the other hand, that if religion is "natural" inasmuch as it has become an adaptive habit, it is nonetheless illusory. Jesse Bering, in *The Belief Instinct*, takes this aggressively atheist line of argument about as far as it will go. Calling God an "adaptive illusion," Bering puts his faith in unguided natural selection to explain everything about us, urging us to see religious belief as "one of natural selection's most successful hoaxes ever." He admits that the findings of cognitive science cannot "disprove the existence of God," but nonetheless insists that "[t]he facts of the evolutionary case imply strongly that God's existence is rather improbable." But even Bering is compelled to regard atheism (which he identifies with "logical thought") as "run[ning] against the grain of our natural psychology."[17]

What, then, are the implications for religious freedom of the cognitive science of religion, if even the most aggressively atheist of its practitioners honestly regards religious belief as wholly natural?

Aristotle famously observed that man is by nature a political animal *because* he is a reasoning animal. The crux of the cognitive-science or anthropological case for religious freedom is that man is by nature a religious animal for much the same reason. As Christian Smith has framed it, human beings are "believing animals." It is as rational beings that they seek an understanding of an ultimate cause that supplies explanations and guidance for their lives.

To repress religion, then, is not to frustrate some odd quirk of human nature, somehow separable from the "true" interests of human beings. Instead, it is to repress the variable yet inevitable religious choices and experiences of actual human beings. Because religious beliefs and social practices have proven so ineradicable, so *natural* in their immense variety and mutability, to repress them is to repress human dignity itself. Religious repression is the denial of the very essence of what it means to be human.

These findings have crucial implications for religious freedom. They mean that the defense of religious freedom is not the defense of an expensive taste or luxury that only a few eccentric and obstinate people happen to indulge. Some people argue precisely along those lines. "Isn't religious freedom advocacy so much special pleading for the special interests and agendas of particular groups," they say, "and doesn't it invent a new, dubious class of human rights that doesn't deserve to take precedence over other human rights?"

At the deepest level, the anthropological case for religious freedom suggests that religious freedom is not special pleading, for the simple reason that religion is not a sideshow in human experience or an incidental feature of human life. Instead, religion is central to human life, enmeshed in human experience, and integral to human fulfillment. Religion is so profoundly intertwined with human existence that it cannot be repressed except at the price of undermining individuality and disrupting society.

To repeat, the cognitive science of religion does not demonstrate the truth of the common intuition that there is a transcendent reality, or of any particular belief about the transcendent. All human beings have the capacity for religious belief, but not all become religious believers. Yet evidence from the cognitive science of religion suggests that the tendency to seek an ultimate order of reality and meaning beyond visible empirical reality is not easily overcome. There seems to be a deeply rooted inclination toward religious yearning embedded in human nature.

It follows from this that it is those who *fail* to promote religious freedom for all people with the same vigor with which they promote freedom of expression, democratic elections, and the rights of women, and those who invent reasons to demote religion to a lower and optional category of rights and freedoms, who are guilty of special pleading. Such persons often defend human rights of every other kind, but find special, *ad hoc* reasons for removing religion from normal democratic protections, or depriving religious persons and communities of rights and freedoms to which they have every claim. This kind of special pleading, sadly, is an equal-opportunity myopia, afflicting conservatives and liberals, Muslims and Christians, Hindus and Buddhists, atheists and the indifferent alike.

The findings of scholars in the cognitive sciences and in the sociology of religion also suggest something important about the public upsurge of religion the world has witnessed in the last several decades, which we will describe more fully in Part Two. The findings suggest that the upsurge is not merely a temporary development but is ultimately rooted in intrinsic features of human experience, and it shows no sign of dissipating. Religion's persistence on the world stage is not simply rooted in contingent circumstances that may well fluctuate, such as demography. It seems to be tied to deep inclinations of human nature and sociability.

To attack the religious practices of human beings is to attack something at the heart of human freedom and of humanity itself. To defend religious freedom is not to engage in special pleading but to defend something important to us all.

Defining Religious Freedom

Religious freedom should be understood . . . not merely as immunity from coercion, but even more fundamentally as an ability to order one's own choices in accordance with truth.

—POPE BENEDICT XVI, MESSAGE FOR THE
WORLD DAY OF PEACE, JANUARY 1, 2011

If religion is the way people strive for harmony with an unseen order of reality, religious freedom is the right to pursue this religious striving in a way that draws on all the dimensions of one's personhood—reason, conscience, will, emotions, body, and soul. It is the freedom to engage one's entire self in pursuit of ultimate reality. This is religious freedom in full.

So defined, religious freedom in full includes at least four major dimensions. First is the freedom of every person to use his reason to seek the truth about whatever unseen order of reality there may be—whether such an order exists and, if so, what its various dimensions might be and what they may say about human life. *It is the religious freedom of intellectual and spiritual inquiry.*

Second, religious freedom in full includes the freedom to engage one's conscience, intellect, and will in embracing whatever truth one can discover about an unseen order of reality. This is the freedom to align one's life with the truth about an unseen order. *It is the religious freedom of practical reason.*

Third, religious freedom in full includes the freedom to engage all the aspects of one's physical being to practice and manifest the truth about the unseen order of reality, and to join with others of like mind and spirit. This is the freedom to speak and act—both individually and in community with others—in ways that express whatever truths one may possess about a transcendent order. *It is the religious freedom of human sociality.*

The fourth and final dimension of religious freedom in full is the right—both individually and as part of a larger religious community—to express religious beliefs freely in civil society and political life on a basis no less favorable than is accorded to non-religious expression. This aspect of religious freedom encompasses the right of religious individuals and groups to own and sell property, or to establish and run religious schools, charitable organizations, and other institutions of civil society. It includes the right to form political parties, or to make arguments in the public square, on the basis of religious teachings. *This is the religious freedom of political and legal expression.*

In sum, a society that treats religion as an eccentricity to be tolerated only for the sake of other considerations *necessarily* does an injustice to its members who rightly judge that religion is a basic aspect of their flourishing, and who organize their lives accordingly. Pope Benedict XVI has observed that religious freedom is not only a negative freedom from coercion but also the positive freedom to organize one's life in accordance with ultimate truth. Because of this positive freedom, "[p]olitical society is morally obliged to create the social space for people to fulfill their obligation to seek the truth in religious matters and live accordingly."[18]

What Religious Freedom Is Not

To say that a person has a right to explore, embrace, and express what his conscience judges to be the truth about a transcendent order of reality, however, is not to make the claim that a person is justified in acting on whatever basis he pleases about religious matters. The right to religious freedom is not a legal right to act on whatever beliefs we fancy about the transcendent, however manifestly evil, illogical, or absurd they may be. Nor does it constitute a right to autonomy of action in a radical sense, as in the alleged right, in the language of the U.S. Supreme Court decision in *Planned Parenthood* v. *Casey*, "to define one's own concept of existence, of meaning, of the universe, and of the mystery of human life."[19]

Furthermore, to claim that there is a right to religious freedom in full is not to claim that all religious doctrines and practices are equally sound, worthy, or true. Instead, to say that a person has a right to religious freedom is to make a claim about the interest or good of the right-holder. Legal philosopher Joseph Raz observes that religious freedom is an individual interest of sufficient weight and of a certain kind that "another" has a duty to act in a way that will serve (or at least not undermine) that individual's interest. Philosopher Nicholas Wolterstorff puts it in a similar way. To say that a person has a right to religious freedom is to say that a certain kind of normative social relationship obtains—the right-holder has a right to the good of being treated in a certain way by others.[20]

In sum, religious freedom constitutes a claim on behalf of persons. It is not a claim that all religions are equally true or that all religion is good for society. Indeed, as we shall see in the next chapter, the case for religious liberty in society and politics rests on the principle of equal access by religious ideas and actors to the political life of the nation, a free and equal contention, as it were, for defining justice and the common good.

CHAPTER TWO

A Political Case for Religious Freedom

*We believe that liberty of religious faith is the first and foremost freedom
in human society, is a universal value in the international community, and
is also the foundation for other political and property rights. Without the
universal and equitable liberty of religious faith, a multi-ethnic, multi-religion
country would not be able to form a peaceful civil society, or bring about
social stability, ethnic solidarity or the nation's prosperity.*

—THE PASTORS OF THE SHOUWANG CHURCH
BEIJING, CHINA, MAY 2011

With this courageous statement, a group of Chinese Christians articulated a
powerful case for religious freedom. After years of government harassment prevented the Shouwang Church from renting or buying a building, police then
forbade church members to hold services in the open air, placing the pastor under
house arrest and detaining other congregants as well. In response, the pastors of
the Shouwang Church sent a petition to the National People's Congress not only
protesting their mistreatment but also insisting on the positive social and political
contributions of religious freedom. Religious freedom, they argued, contributes to
peaceful civil society, social stability, ethnic solidarity, and national prosperity.

These Chinese citizens made a *political* case for religious freedom. That is, they
argued that their society and political order would flourish only to the extent that
they protected religious freedom. They advocated this right not for the sake of being
defiant, and not only to promote the interests of their own Christian community.
As one young member of the church told *Washington Post* columnist Michael
Gerson, the congregation is mainly "intellectuals and professionals" who "respect
the government, love the country, respect authority."[21] These people see themselves
as having a stake in their country's future. Their argument for religious freedom
was made at least in part for the sake of their society and its common good.

Religious freedom, we contend, can contribute to security, stability, freedom, prosperity, the equality of women, and other social, economic, and political goods. Religious repression, on the other hand, tends to foster violence, instability, tyranny, economic stagnation, and female oppression. As we shall see in Part Two, the political case for religious freedom substantially overlaps with the strategic case.

Religious freedom in full, as noted, entails that set of institutions, laws, and habits that yield equality under the law for all religious actors and ideas. It does not rest merely on the absence of persecution or restrictions. Rather, it requires the presence of a mutually reinforcing web of government protections, established freedoms, and social norms and practices.

Equality under the law affords all religious individuals and communities an equal right to conduct private or semi-private activities normally protected in a functioning democracy—for example, the right to believe or not, the right to enter or exit religious communities, the right (within broad limits) to build houses of worship, train clergy, raise children in the faith, build religious schools, establish disciplinary norms for membership, and invite others to join the religious community.

Equality under the law also affords equal access by religious actors to the legal, political, and economic institutions and processes of a state. This means that they may, for example, form democratic political parties on the basis of religious teachings, purchase property, receive charitable donations, or run charitable organizations. It means they may publicly articulate norms of justice and the common good, and seek to influence or change laws and public policies, based on their teachings. It means that all individuals may run for public office, regardless of their faith, membership in a religious community, or holding of a religious office.

No society can become fully free by protests, elections, and constitutional referenda alone. Without religious freedom in full, democracy is unlikely to be stable and lasting. This is true in at least three senses.

First, societies lacking full religious liberty lack a critical restriction on state power. When citizens are free to have an ultimate commitment to something more than human, something beyond the authorities of society and state, the power of the state is thereby limited.

Second, religiously unfree societies often generate disorder. The impulse to attach oneself to something above society and the state seems to be an ineradicable feature of human nature, so much so that systematic efforts to suppress that impulse will often lead to insecurity and violence.

Third, a democratic polity based on religious freedom in full imposes a discipline on religious ideas and actors. While it invites those ideas and actors into civic and political life, it requires them to accept the constraints imposed by the foundational principle of equality under the law—for other religious communities, whether majority or minority, and for non-religious ideas and groups. Democracy imposes on all its religious citizens and associations the limits and norms of democracy itself.

Religious Liberty Is Tightly Bundled with Other Liberties

Social science confirms that religious liberty is tightly bundled with other liberties. If a society cares about having these other liberties, it should care about ensuring religious freedom. In a sense, religious liberty is the thin end of liberty's wedge: the deeper religious liberty is driven and embedded, the more a society is opened up to a wide range of other liberties.

Because of what they stand to lose, authoritarian governments sometimes have a keener sense of this dynamic than others. In response to the efforts of the Shouwang Church to win its freedom, the Chinese government implicitly acknowledged the deep political significance of that claim. After the crackdown on the Shouwang Church, the state-owned *Global Times* newspaper commented, "a church should not become a power which can promote radical change. . . . Otherwise, the church is not engaged in religion but in politics, which is not allowed for a church."[22] In short, the Chinese government seeks to suppress this church and all other religious communities because it fears their ability to exercise political and civil influence in Chinese society.

Why should China's government fear the influence of religious communities on Chinese society? Sociologist Brian Grim's work suggests a persuasive answer. Religious liberty is "bundled" with other liberties that tend to undermine all statist regimes:

> Religious freedom is embedded within a much larger bundle of civil liberties. At the core of religious expression is the freedom of speech and at the core of freedom to worship is the freedom to assemble. To claim freedom of speech without allowing for a freedom to express religious beliefs quickly erodes freedom of speech in other areas. Likewise, allowing for restrictions on the assembly of religious groups opens the door for curtailing the activities of other groups as well. The denial of religious freedom is inevitably intertwined with the denial of other freedoms.[23]

Grim's analysis of some recent data on religious freedom demonstrates a strong relationship between religious liberty and a variety of political and civil liberties. The figure below graphically illustrates the strength of this relationship.

In the chart, the size of each number and the area of each corresponding pie slice indicate the strength of the direct correlation with religious liberty. All the correlations are statistically significant, which is to say that there is some clear relationship between religious freedom and the other identified categories. The chart demonstrates that the relationship between religious freedom and political freedom, freedom of the press, and other civil liberties is particularly robust. Grim notes that the strong and highly significant correlations suggest that these freedoms are closely intertwined.

FIGURE I: Correlation of religious liberty with other liberties and aspects of societal well-being.*

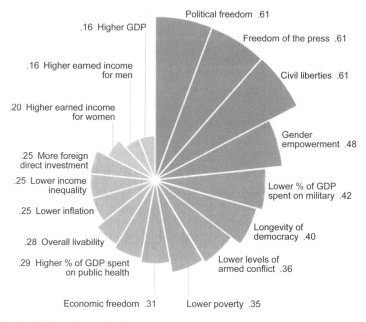

*This figure is from Brian J. Grim and Roger Finke, *The Price of Freedom Denied: Religious Persecution and Conflict in the 21st Century* (New York: Cambridge University Press, 2011), 206, and is used here with the permission of the authors.

According to Grim, other research provides independent confirmation of these findings. Using its own independent data, the Center for Religious Freedom of the Hudson Institute analyzed the relationship between religious liberty and other liberties in 101 countries. The Hudson Institute study found that religious liberty is powerfully associated with civil and political liberty, press freedom, economic freedom, and prolonged democracy.[24]

Of course, even a strong correlation does not mean causation. It could be that religious freedom is the product of other democratic forces, rather than a contributing cause of democratic development. But there is significant evidence that religious liberty is more than a mere byproduct of other democratizing factors. At the very least, it appears to be central to the bundled group of fundamental freedoms that enable democracy to take root and to endure. The evidence suggests that, especially in highly religious societies, democracy and its many economic, social, and political benefits are unlikely to be sustained over time without religious freedom.[25]

The value of religious freedom to democracy also rests on certain democratic norms. Framed in terms of the limits proper to a free, democratic state, the argument is that every government should consider itself accountable to principles and realities above and beyond society and the state.

Any government that presumes to direct how its people relate to ultimate truths either believes it is the only guide to those truths, or that government itself is the source of truth and its citizens must believe that nothing exists beyond the material world. To dictate human beings' relation to the transcendent is to lower the horizons of political life by rendering it entirely self-justifying—a law unto itself. This is the end of democracy and the beginning of tyranny.

To deny freedom of religion is not only to diminish the dignity of individual persons, but also to diminish the integrity and justice of society itself—turning it from something that responds to an authority higher than itself, into something that is merely self-referential. A government that prevents its people from seeking an authority beyond the state, or that presumes to tell them precisely where it is to be found, has lost any claim to being a democratic or free regime.

Religious Freedom Cuts Short Vicious Cycles of Alienation, Repression, and Violence

It is also true that no society lacking full religious freedom can be free from the threat of disorder and insecurity. Human nature is such that its horizons cannot be completely defined or confined by the laws, conventions, and mores of any single society. When a state seeks to limit the horizons of what it means to be human and to live a good life, people will find a way to resist, sometimes by violence.

Brian Grim and Roger Finke have analyzed the trends in religious freedom in nearly every country in the world, based on the voluminous reports produced by the U.S. State Department as well as numerous other sources. What they have found is that "to the extent that governments deny religious freedoms, violent religious persecution and conflict will increase." Conversely, they found that "when religious freedoms are granted to all religions, the state has less *authority* and fewer *incentives* to persecute religion."[26]

Contrasting empirical cases illustrate these dynamics. Consider the differences between Sudan and Tajikistan. In Sudan, the Khartoum government's assertion that Islamic law should govern all of Sudan has been a major catalyst in Sudan's perennial and horrific violence since the 1950s. In autumn 1983, the Nimeiri government imposed the "September laws," which made Sharia the basis of the national legal system. The government's forced imposition of Sharia throughout all of Sudan, even in those areas with non-Muslim populations, pushed religion into the center of Sudanese politics and helped to spark the second civil war between the north and the south (the first one having occurred from the 1950s to the early 1970s). Today there is a tenuous peace in Sudan only because the south has been permitted to secede from the north.[27]

Tajikistan's own civil war began much the same way, except the repressive state was a neo-communist secular government. It refused to cede power to the combined opposition of nationalists, Islamists, and democrats. According to political scientist Mohammed Hafez, "indiscriminate repression against anyone suspected of supporting the opposition . . . produced hundreds of thousands of refugees, from whom the ranks of the rebels were recruited."[28] After tens of thousands of people were killed in a civil war in the early 1990s, a peace agreement included an offer of amnesty and legalization of the Islamist parties. Specifically, the state decided to accommodate the Islamic Renaissance Party and assign it a place in the political process. In contrast to the repressive policies and simmering tensions in neighboring countries such as Turkmenistan, Uzbekistan, and Kyrgyzstan, "the incorporation of a formally armed opposition into [Tajikistan's] power structures along with the emergence of a moderate Islamic party represents an indisputable success."[29]

This aspect of the political case for religious freedom can also be framed in terms of the integrity of society. Any state or culture that coerces the consciences of its members in religious matters invites the hostility and alienation of those it is coercing. Such a system does not produce a stable uniformity but suppresses and masks an inevitable diversity of religious beliefs and expressions, and can be sustained over the long run only by intensifying coercion.

Of course, most repressive governments hold that the stability of their societies depends upon the maintenance of tight *controls* on religious liberty—as well as other freedoms of the individual and of associations. Political scientist Anthony Gill has usefully reminded us that religious liberty *is* destabilizing to settled political orders in which it has not previously appeared. New entrants into the "religious economy" will compete for adherents, and sometimes engender conflict among competing faith groups or between some of those groups and the state. Gill then asks whether destabilization is likely to be perennial:

> Are we then relegated to a situation wherein we must always tolerate high levels of conflict if we want acceptably high levels of freedom? Not necessarily. Once new entrants become entrenched, social conflict and violence will become an increasingly counter-productive strategy for the dominant religious group, and it is likely that the government will not tolerate it since intensified conflict is economically counter-productive and has the potential to be politically destabilizing. . . . In essence, and to put it in terms familiar to those studying international relations, when there is a stable balance of power, or when you arrive at a situation where no one single religion is dominant, you are much more likely to develop a relatively calm and stable situation of religious pluralism.[30]

The protection of religious freedom, Gill argues, is a dynamic thing. Religion itself is such a powerful force in people's lives that we should not be surprised to learn that according religious freedom in full to all citizens can be disorienting and destabilizing. But the journey of freedom, from destructive conflict to peaceful competition among religious faiths, is the only way forward for societies that seek stability, prosperity, and a flourishing civil society. In the end, ordered liberty *works*. Authoritarian repression, whether by governments captured by one dominant religion or by governments hostile to religion as such, constitutes an injustice to human dignity. It is also a sure path to a stunted civil society and permanent instability.

The health and wholeness of every society, we argue, depend on fully protecting religious freedom. Whatever we call this characteristic of the political community—"societal integrity" or "civic integrity" or something else—it requires that all religious believers enjoy the rights to independence and vigorous social and political involvement.

As understood and as articulated here, therefore, religious freedom is a foundational political freedom, in at least three senses. It is a freedom that every government is duty-bound to embrace and promote as a first principle of political order. It is a freedom that imposes limits on every political order—i.e., restraints and checks against every government, and on its religious actors (on the same basis as its non-religious actors). And it is a freedom that is essential to the integrity and flourishing of every political community. Religious freedom is a foundational principle of political society, an inviolable limit on political society, and an immense benefit to political society.

CHAPTER THREE

A Moral Case for Religious Freedom

*The exercise of conscience—the making of the moral judgments
that is necessary to these enterprises—and the pursuit of religion . . .
have a claim to be the most central aspects of an agent's
attempts at upright self-constitution, aspects which, if intruded
upon in unreasonable ways, would cut to the heart of an agent's
ability to act, and constitute herself as, a person.*

—CHRISTOPHER TOLLEFSEN, PROFESSOR OF PHILOSOPHY,
UNIVERSITY OF SOUTH CAROLINA

In giving an account above of religion's rootedness in human nature, hence an anthropological case for religious freedom, we found it unavoidable to speak in moral language about our conclusions. After all, what presents itself as fundamentally woven into the fabric of our consciousness—that an unseen order makes its demand on our attention, just as do the minds of others whom we can see—seems to be a matter of utmost moral gravity. Even if most of the men and women who have ever lived—or all of them—could be shown to have been mistaken about the existence and character of a transcendent order above or behind the world our senses can detect, our intuitive moral sense would still whisper in our ears that the freedom to pursue the truth for ourselves is one of mankind's most precious possessions.

But an intuitive moral sense will not do, in the end. The same anthropological insights tell us that human beings are capable of a relentlessly rational skepticism, and must be presented with *reasons* for a moral conclusion about religious freedom. And the political considerations discussed above will not meet the case, either, for one might reasonably think that the price of imperfectly suppressed social conflict is not too high to pay, if justice can be shown to demand the suppression of religious diversity and dissent from a state-enforced orthodoxy.

Not "Cultural" But Universal

What then, is the case in moral philosophy for religious freedom? We must begin by noting that such a case necessarily transcends any particular society's norms. Religious freedom is not rooted in mere convention, though it is undeniable that the conventions of particular peoples have sometimes accurately reflected and helpfully clarified the rationale of religious freedom.

And we are confident that religious freedom is a principle, not because it is affirmed in Article 18 of the Universal Declaration of Human Rights—as compelling a statement as it is. Rather, the Universal Declaration expresses the truth that religious freedom is a universal demand of justice—a truth we know independently of the conventions and laws of any particular society or epoch.

In a joint press conference with China's president Hu Jintao on January 19, 2011, President Barack Obama cast a bright if inadvertent spotlight on just these questions. The president spoke of "the universal rights of every human being," and went on to specify religious freedom as among the most prominent of these universal rights. "We have some core views, as Americans," President Obama insisted, "about the universality of certain rights—freedom of speech, freedom of religion, freedom of assembly—that we think are very important and that transcend cultures."[31]

Though President Obama's remarks were admirable for their clarity, particularly as he stood next to the president of a country that is one of the world's worst violators of religious freedom, he arguably conveyed two contradictory messages: on the one hand, that religious freedom is a "universal" right, and, on the other hand, that it is a peculiarly American right. So again: if religious freedom is a right, what sort of right is it? If it is a "universal right" that "transcends cultures," what is its basis? What is it grounded in? Or is a high view of religious freedom merely a parochial perspective reflecting the "core views" of "Americans"?

We argue that religious freedom is a universal right because it is based on considerations that are, in principle, as accessible to non-Americans as to Americans, to non-Christians as to Christians, and to non-Westerners as to Westerners. We also argue that religious freedom is not based on peculiarly American or Western principles or philosophies, such as liberalism or individualism. (Of course, this is not to deny that religious freedom is "American" in the sense that it is fundamentally important in the American constitutional order.)

The path to defining a universal foundation for the right to religious freedom in full is through a series of steps that are firmly rooted in human experience. We have already taken a few of these steps—anthropological and political. A further stepping-stone is moral. It is the nature and dignity of the *human person*. Religious freedom rests on this stepping-stone in ways that genuinely "transcend cultures," in the apt words of President Obama.

What, then, is the source of the universal right to religious freedom?

The Dignity and Integrity of the Human Person

The dignity and integrity of the human person require that all people everywhere enjoy the freedom to fulfill their duty to seek and embrace the truth about transcendent reality as best they can.

Human beings are noble agents—agents with high worth and dignity. An integral aspect of these characteristics is that all persons have the great privilege and responsibility of freely forming their own judgments of reason and conscience about—and freely establishing their own relationship with—transcendent reality.

They have an intrinsic interest in forming their characters and lives—constituting themselves—into integrated wholes that fully reflect the demands and implications of transcendent truth as they grasp it. Anything less than full religious freedom fails to respect the dignity of persons as free truth-seekers, duty-bound to respond to the truth (and only the truth) about the transcendent in accordance with their own judgments of conscience. Furthermore, anything less than full religious freedom also fails to respect the proper integrity and authenticity of persons.

What persons gain, therefore, when they enjoy religious freedom is the freedom to make judgments concerning religious truths in accordance with their own dictates of conscience, not in accordance with the dictates of some coercive, external authority. What they gain, as well, is the freedom to act on these judgments in the way they organize their personal lives and in the way they express themselves in their communities. What they gain is the full freedom to be persons.

Conversely, what they lose when they do not enjoy religious freedom is the freedom to make and act on their own judgments of religious conscience. In losing this freedom, they lose capacities that are essential to being complete human beings.

When people lose their religious freedom, in other words, they lose more than their freedom to be religious. They lose their freedom to be human.

The dignity of human beings, then, grounds the various dimensions of religious freedom: the freedom to explore the truth about an unseen order, the freedom to embrace it, and the freedom to express it.

A Right to Explore the Truth About an Unseen Order

If human dignity requires that people be free to explore the truth about transcendent reality, they possess a right to immunity and security from coercive or manipulative interference by others.

Religious freedom also entails duties. "Conscience has rights," in John Henry Newman's pithy observation, "because it has duties."[32] If a transcendent order exists, then it imposes a supremely important duty on each of us to discover all we can about its nature, as well as to achieve whatever harmony with it we can. It is self-evident that if truth about ultimate reality in fact exists, it is of paramount moral and practical importance. The knowledge of such truth would be singularly illuminating both of what is *real* and of how we should live our lives. The supreme importance of this knowledge imposes a supreme duty: to form our consciences and orient our lives in accordance with whatever truths we can gather about its nature and demands.

Efforts to coerce or manipulate us into adopting a particular religious opinion—even when based on the premise that the religious opinion being imposed is true, and even when animated by the best of intentions—are intrinsically unsuited to helping us see the truth of the opinion. They are, one might say, incapable of helping us see the truth *as* true. When truth appears at the point of a gun or as the condition of a bribe, then the truth and its bearers will appear doubtful if not repellent and hateful to us—in other words, as anything but the truth. "I endure not an instructor that comes to me under the wardship of an overseeing fist," insisted John Milton.[33] For if the "truth" requires such instruments for its "communication," how can it be true? "When a religion is good, I conceive it will support itself," reasoned Benjamin Franklin, "and when it does not support itself, and God does not take care to support it so that its professors are obliged to call for help of the civil power, 'tis a sign, I apprehend, of its being a bad one."[34]

We can imagine two purposes of coercion. One is to promote religious opinions that are false and to suppress religious opinions that are true. In this case, coercion is manifestly destructive and damaging to the duty to explore transcendent truth. Such a policy keeps truth out of sight, unexplored, and unembraced. The other purpose is to promote religious opinions that are true and to suppress religious opinions that are false. In this case, coercion is likely to "succeed" only in making "good" religion appear "bad," as Franklin suggested. We might add that it is likely to succeed in making "bad" religion look martyred and heroic. "[I]nstead of suppressing sects and schisms," argues Milton, "[coercion] raises them and invests them with a reputation." Either way, coercive interference distorts and inhibits the exploration of the truth about transcendent reality.

A Right to Embrace the Truth About an Unseen Order

Religious freedom protects the efforts of human beings to embrace the truth about transcendent reality. Here again, conscience has rights because it has duties. If after a process of exploring the truth about transcendent reality, we firmly, finally, and sincerely believe that we have grasped the truth about transcendent reality, then we have a duty to embrace it and constitute ourselves in accordance with its demands.

This is what is meant by conscience: it is not a mysterious, extra-rational faculty, but the best and final judgment of our reason concerning what is true. "Conscience is a judgment of reason," Christopher Tollefsen explains, "and an upright will acts in accordance with reason."[35] Whatever one's conscience judges to be the truth about transcendent reality, one's duty is to align his will, emotions, dispositions, and choices with its implications.

We have such a duty, it should be emphasized, even in the event that we are mistaken. If we judge that we have grasped the truth about transcendent reality, but what we judge to be true is in fact false, it remains the case that we can discharge our duty to the truth only by embracing what we judge to be true. Of course, we are obligated to seek the truth "in good faith," attempting to form our consciences with diligence and noble purpose, for to do otherwise would be to fail in our duty.

Because we have a duty to embrace what we take to be the truth about transcendent reality, because of our interest in the truth and in acting with integrity, it follows that we have a right to be secure from the attempts of others to block or hinder us from embracing what we believe to be the truth. So, too, we have the right to be free from active interference by others—including attempts to punish or abuse us—in our efforts to align our lives and priorities with the truth.

A Right to Express the Truth About an Unseen Order

Finally, the right to religious freedom requires that we be free to express the truth about transcendent reality to other persons and in society.

If we believe that we possess even a part of the truth about transcendent reality, then to be prevented from expressing this truth outwardly and publicly is to suffer in at least three ways.

First, we are unable to do justice to the truth. We are not able to express our loyalty and adherence to the truth.

Second, we are unable to do justice to ourselves and our own integrity. We are unable to be authentic, and fail to make our actions "genuine realizations of our own freely ordered evaluations, preferences, hopes, and self-determination."[36]

Third, we are unable to do justice to other persons. If we believe we are in possession of the truth about transcendent reality, then we have a duty to share it with others for the sake of their well-being.

The freedom to express and manifest the truth about transcendent reality has communal and public dimensions. Because persons are social and inclined to seek the truth about transcendent reality, they naturally band together to deepen their understanding of transcendent truth and jointly manifest it to others. Attacks on religious communities, therefore, on their rights to assemble or to manifest and propagate their distinctive message, are attacks on the sociability and communal nature of persons, attacks on the interest of human persons in authentic self-constitution, and attacks on the good of religion.

Thus individuals and communities of all faiths, or of none, enjoy two basic rights. One is the right to an autonomous social existence, free of unwarranted suppression or intrusion by government or other social actors. The other is the right to full civic and political participation, equal to that of other citizens and social or political actors.

An imposition of secular orthodoxy—denying the right of full civic and political participation—would be unjust because it would amount to an attack on the integrity of religious believers, many of whom consider their faith intertwined with every aspect of their lives, public and private.

Robust religious freedom necessarily entails a two-dimensional civic freedom. It is the right of religious individuals and groups to practice their religion, privately and publicly, and the right of religious individuals and groups to speak in their own voice—to contribute their own distinctive message to social and political life.

Religious freedom, then, is the freedom of human will, reason, and conscience, of human souls and spirits, to explore and embrace whatever they can discover concerning the origin and meaning of all things and of all reality. It is the freedom of *who we are* to embrace the ultimate truth about *all that is*. Whether "alone" or "in community," whether in "private" or in "public," as the Universal Declaration emphasizes, it is our freedom to hold and manifest what we believe to be true about the deepest realities and highest things.

All persons enjoy an inalienable right to religious freedom because of their nature and dignity as persons, because of the dignity and integrity of religion, and because of the dignity and integrity of society. Every person has an intrinsic and universal interest in his own dignity and integrity, an intrinsic and universal interest in the dignity and integrity of religion, and an intrinsic and universal interest in the dignity and integrity of his society. These goods are not merely instrumental to our well-being but are intrinsic to it. They are not merely useful to some higher goal or larger happiness but are integral to any meaningful concept or experience of human fulfillment.

Religious freedom is fundamental to the life of each person—to each one *as* a person, *and* as a respondent to religious duty, *and* as a bearer of the right so to respond in his society. On the basis of these universal foundations, we can be confident in claiming that all people everywhere ought to enjoy a fundamental right to religious freedom.

CHAPTER FOUR

A Religious Case for Religious Freedom

*[I]f there is a God . . . it can be expected a priori that He
wants a voluntary response born of genuine gratitude and
humility themselves rooted in reflection and morally responsible
choice. Seen in this light, heresy and even apostasy are morally
more acceptable than any hypocritical attachment to
orthodox opinion out of the fear of public sanctions.*

—SHABBIR AKHTAR, MUSLIM PHILOSOPHER

It is commonly argued that, in the defense of religious freedom, appeals to religion itself are somehow illegitimate. Religious freedom, it is argued, must be grounded in, and defended on the basis of, "secular" reasoning about "tolerance" or about the sheer "necessity" of having to get along with others in a pluralistic environment. Religion itself cannot supply a ground for religious freedom, for its own native inclinations are toward irrational fanaticism and coercion. And so, in this line of thinking, the last place to look for strong support for religious liberty is in the convictions and traditions of religious believers themselves.

Without denying that ideas outside religion can play a valuable and perhaps even necessary role in nudging religious traditions and communities toward a healthy respect for liberty and toleration, there is also a powerful *religious* case for religious freedom. Throughout history, after all, alongside undeniable instances of religion-inspired persecution, tyranny, and fanaticism, there have been equally undeniable instances of religion-inspired movements for fundamental human rights, toleration, and freedom.

Such advocacy has often focused on religious liberty. From the early church father Lactantius in the fourth century, to Roger Williams, the Protestant dissenter and founder of Rhode Island in the seventeenth century, and up to the contemporary Muslim theologian and president of Indonesia, the late Abdurrahman Wahid, numerous religious thinkers and statesmen have advanced a capacious concept of religious freedom on expressly religious grounds. Speaking for many faith-based advocates of religious toleration, Richard John Neuhaus observed that "[i]t is not chiefly a secular but a religious restraint that prevents biblical believers from coercing others in matters of conscience. . . . [W]e believe that it is the will of God that we should not kill one another over our disagreements about the will of God."[37]

The purpose of this section is not to survey how various religious figures have made a case for religious liberty in history, or to discuss the influence of their advocacy in particular contexts. Instead, its purpose is to summarize some leading religious arguments for religious freedom. These arguments are of two kinds.

The first may be called phenomenological. This argument proceeds not from any particular religion or theological tradition but from the nature of religion as such. As we have argued, religion is the intrinsically worthwhile human activity of seeking some understanding of, and harmony with, whatever transcendent order of reality there might be. The question is: does reflection on this human phenomenon or human activity, in and of itself, require respect for religious freedom?

The answer is emphatically "yes." The nature of religion itself requires that the religious conviction and expression of all people be free from coercive interference and manipulation. One reason is that religion is a basic component of human flourishing, a fundamental good. As such, religious freedom deserves the respect and deference of every human being and every human authority. A second reason is that religious belief and practice must be free and uncoerced if they are to be authentic.

The second kind of religious argument for religious freedom may be called theological. This kind of argument proceeds from particular religious traditions. It is not general or phenomenological but necessarily specific, arising from reflection on the scriptures and authorities that are distinctive to particular religious traditions. The particularity of theological argument, however, presents a challenge: can one usefully summarize important theological arguments for religious freedom deriving from the world's theological systems and traditions, which are characterized by great diversity? It is hazardous to try.

To minimize (though by no means eliminate) the hazard, we invited three prominent scholars, one Jewish, one Christian, and one Muslim, to summarize some of the leading theological arguments for religious freedom that emerge from their respective religious traditions. Rather than try to summarize the relevant doctrines of all the major "world religions," we seek to convey a sense of how three important religious traditions offer significant grounds for respecting religious freedom—and do so as a matter of principle, not merely of prudence. These perspectives are offered by Jewish theologian David Novak, Christian philosopher Nicholas Wolterstorff, and Muslim philosopher Abdullah Saeed. Without claiming to speak with authority for any community, they offer clear reasons for seeing that principles favoring religious freedom are close to the heart of each of these three great religious traditions.

Taken together, the various phenomenological and theological arguments for religious freedom converge in a remarkable way around a core proposition—namely, that faith is not faith unless it is free. The core religious argument for religious freedom, then, is that freedom is religion's essential precondition. Coercion in matters of faith does not merely violate religion. It nullifies religion. Freedom for faith does not merely honor religion. It is what makes religion possible.

The Nature of Religion as Special and Valuable Requires Respect for Religious Freedom

Respect for religious freedom as a basic right must begin in respectful acknowledgment that all people may be in a prior relationship with a transcendent order of reality, and that each has a basic interest in exploring whether there is such an order and in discovering what it might be. Apart from such an acknowledgment, religious freedom has little hope of being secure.

James Madison famously made the point in 1785:

> It is the duty of every man to render to the Creator such homage and such only as he believes to be acceptable to him. *This duty is precedent, both in order of time and in degree of obligation, to the claims of Civil Society. Before any man can be considered as a member of Civil Society, he must be considered as a subject of the Governour of the Universe*: And if a member of Civil Society, who enters into any subordinate Association, must always do it with a reservation of his duty to the General Authority; much more must every man who becomes a member of any particular Civil Society, do it with a saving of his allegiance to the Universal Sovereign. We maintain therefore that in matters of Religion, no mans [sic] right is abridged by the institution of Civil Society and that Religion is wholly exempt from its cognizance.[38]

Though Madison frames the argument in terms of a personal God, the argument does not depend on a theistic framework. In Sophocles' *Antigone*, the eponymous heroine insists that she must give her brother a decent burial—against the orders of the tyrannical king Creon. "I owe a longer allegiance to the dead than to the living," Antigone reasons, for "in that world I shall abide for ever." If our conscience persuades us that a "world" beyond this one truly exists in some sense, then it is reasonable to conclude, like Antigone, that we owe this transcendent order a stronger allegiance than any we owe in this world.

If religion offers even the possibility of some acquaintance or harmony with ultimate reality, even some finite grasp of infinite truth, then it is an enterprise that deserves the respectful deference Creon declined to show Antigone.

Of course, to say that the nature of religion requires that the religious freedom of all persons be accorded presumptive respect is not to say that the actual religious activities of human beings are all equally valuable and equally deserving of respect and deference. Consider an analogy to marriage and family life. Marriage and the integrity of family life are basic goods that deserve the protection of society. This claim does not mean that particular marriages and families do not sometimes assume such destructive forms that the normal deference to family privacy ceases to apply. Where the state normally has a compelling interest in promoting marriage and family, it may be required in some cases to enforce a judicial separation or even a restraining order to protect one spouse (or ex-spouse) from the other. Where the state normally defers to parental authority, it may be required in some cases to remove children from parental custody in order to protect the former from grave danger. So, too, with religion. The fact that the nature of religion as an intrinsically worthwhile activity deserves presumptive deference does not mean that all religious activities deserve the protection of society.

Why should we think religion as such is especially worthy? Relatively few people in human history have even attempted to demonstrate that religion *qua* religion is an entirely worthless and futile enterprise. And no one has offered a conclusive demonstration that no divinity can possibly exist, or that there is no transcendent reality, or that the truth about them is unreachable. One might even suggest that in the Western world today, even after decades of earnest efforts by countless philosophers unfriendly to religion, "atheology" or "anti-theology" shows signs of being on the defensive to a degree that was unforeseeable twenty-five or fifty years ago.

If an ultimate reality—an unseen and perhaps divine order of things—may in fact exist, then it is entirely reasonable for human beings to seek to know that reality and to live in harmony with it. As Christopher Tollefsen explains,

> any human being, thinking clearly about the range of possibilities that could make them well off will recognize that being right with— i.e., conforming one's will to—whatever greater than human source of meaning there might be is an intelligibly attractive possibility.[39]

This intelligibly attractive possibility is the good of religion.

The very nature of religion, then, imposes duties on society. The first duty is that it refrain from degrading religion by denying the possibility of transcendent, religious truth or by subjecting religion to unwarranted control.

The second duty flows from the fact that religion requires freedom in order to be authentic. A precondition of anyone's apprehending whatever truths religion may impart is that it be free and uncoerced. The more religion is subject to external interference, the less it is authentically religious, and the less it is capable of contributing to human fulfillment.

If there is a transcendent source of all that is, no one can weigh the evidence for us and come to a conclusion about its nature and identity. If there is a divine reality, no one can respond to it for us. If we are to participate in the good of religion, apprehending and appropriating for ourselves its truths and benefits, then we must each respond to the truth about the transcendent.

To put it another way, religion is a reflexive good. Religion is not a commodity that can be doled out to us, like food. Nor is it a public good that can be procured and safeguarded for us and our fellow citizens, like clean air or public safety. If necessary, we can be fed against our will, and our bodies can receive all the nourishment food can give whether or not we receive it willingly—whether or not we choose to receive it through the cooperation of our will and reason. (A prisoner threatening a hunger strike unto death can, if necessary, be fed intravenously against his will.) Each of us enjoys the benefits of clean air and safe streets regardless of whether we engage our conscience and deliberative faculties and "choose" to receive or appropriate these benefits. We benefit whether or not we choose to benefit.

Not so with religion. Even where the religion in question is true, we cannot fully receive and absorb its truths unless we engage and grasp it by means of our own will and understanding.

Violations of religious freedom also dishonor the dignity of religion and of any divine reality. They presume to dictate how individuals should understand and relate to the divine reality, or prohibit any such relation altogether, and they make it difficult—often by design—for anyone influenced by them to undertake a sincere and conscientious effort to establish harmony with the divine reality based on truth, freedom, and conscience, rather than fear, coercion, and convention.

From a religious perspective, one might reasonably hold that the divine reality cannot be pleased by any "piety" stunted by coercive fear or convention. Here is the early church father Tertullian:

> See that you do not give a reason for impious religious practice by taking away religious liberty (*libertatem religionis*) and prohibit choice (*optione*) in divine matters, so that I may not worship as I wish (*velim*), but am forced to worship what I do not wish. *No one wishes to be venerated unwillingly, not even a human being (Nemo se ab invite coli volet, ne homo quidem).*[40]

Elisha Williams, rector of Yale in the early eighteenth century, put this insight in Christian terms, but it would hold as well for any view that a divine reality exercises sovereign authority over the human conscience:

> [I]f Christ be the Lord of the conscience, the sole King in his own kingdom; then it will follow, that all such as in any manner or degree assume the power of directing and governing the consciences of men, are justly chargeable with invading his rightful dominion; He alone having the right they claim. Should the king of France take it into his head to prescribe laws to the subjects of the king of Great Britain;

who would not say, it was an invasion of and insult offer'd to the British legislature.[41]

If there is a divine reality of a personal character, any attempt to coerce the path of piety to follow one course rather than another—or to stifle it altogether—must be considered not only a grave threat to human dignity but also a grave injustice to the dignity of religion and to the dignity of that transcendent reality.

A Jewish Case for Religious Freedom, by David Novak

To understand how religious liberty operates in Judaism, one must see its roots in the Jewish dogma of the election of Israel—namely, that God has elected the Jewish people for a special covenantal relationship with Godself. This dogma largely determines the relations of Jews with themselves and with the non-Jewish world. These two relations are different, just as God is related to the Jewish people differently than God is related to all other peoples.

Usually, when one thinks of religious liberty, it pertains to the rights or claims of a minority religious community upon the majority religious community, among whom they live and who have power over them. Minimally, they ask the majority not to prevent them from practicing their religion. Here the minority seems to be asking for legal toleration. Maximally, religious liberty is their claim on the majority community to aid the minority community in the affirmation and practice of their religion. Here the minority seems to be asking for respect.

According to the Talmud, in ancient Israel non-Jews were allowed to live freely among Jews, and these non-Jewish "resident aliens" were not required to convert to Judaism in order to gain the right of permanent residence in the Jewish polity. All that was required of them was their formal acceptance of the basic moral norms that the Jewish tradition regarded to be already binding on all human beings from creation, which the Jewish tradition calls the "Noahide commandments" (Noah being the progenitor of all humankind after the Flood). By acceptance of these duties, they gained the civil rights and privileges we associate with citizenship in a constitutional state. And, even though such a non-Jewish candidate for this kind of second-class citizenship in the Jewish polity also had to renounce idolatry, it seems that this requirement was only enforced in cases of conspicuous idolatry, which might attract some of the Jewish majority away from their covenant with God toward the worship of other gods.

Furthermore, even though Jews did not have this kind of political power over non-Jews until the establishment of the State of Israel in 1948, nevertheless, beginning in the Middle Ages, most Jewish theologians argued that this kind of renunciation of idolatry would not be required of Christians and Muslims, since they have already renounced idolatry when their formerly pagan adherents moved from polytheism to monotheism. And, even though the State of Israel is not governed by traditional Jewish law (*halakhah*), its granting the right of religious liberty to Christians and Muslims living under its rule is quite consistent with the stance of most of the tradition on the rights of non-Jews.

All of this seems to follow from the dogma of the election of Israel. For, whereas Judaism does not recognize Jews having any right to choose whether to be Jews or not, non-Jews do have the right to choose whether or not they want to live in a Jewish society as non-Jews, even as non-Jews practicing a non-Jewish religion. But non-Jews do not have the liberty to violate the Noahide commandments with impunity. Just as the Jews may not choose to reject their covenantal status because God has chosen them for this status, so non-Jews may not choose to reject basic moral law because God has created them to be morally responsible beings. Both statutes, then, are rooted in divine election. God has chosen to create humans in God's image, which the Talmud interprets to mean that all humans are subject to divine law, which is known to be authoritative even before the divine revelation to the Jews at Sinai. And God has chosen the Jews, which makes God's relations with all other peoples quite different.

Religious liberty is more complicated, however, when it pertains to inter-Jewish relations. Due to the primacy of God's indelible election of the Jewish people, and of all individual Jews by virtue of their birth (or "rebirth" through conversion) into the Jewish people, Judaism does not recognize the right of any Jew to leave the Jewish people by becoming part of another people though conversion to their religion. The principle here is: "Even a Jew who has sinned [even the sin of apostasy] is still considered to be a Jew." Thus conversion to another religion is the exercise of an unjustified right and does not change the status of any Jews who exercise this illegitimate right—at least metaphysically, in the divine scheme of things.

Nevertheless, in practice, there are some definite political changes when a Jew does choose to convert to another religion. In effect, that person loses almost all of what are considered the basic privileges of being a Jew, and the Jewish community is therefore not required to exercise responsibility for such an apostate. In fact, the only privilege such an apostate retains is his right to return to the community by the simultaneous repentance of the sin of apostasy. Accordingly, the community is required to take that Jew back, and it rarely imposes any penalty for his past transgression. Moreover, part of the community's renunciation of responsibility for apostates is *that it does not coerce an apostate back into the community. Indeed, this can be seen to be* de facto *recognition of the political (though not theological) liberty right of the apostate.*

This procedural decision (however tacitly made) can be seen to have been greatly influenced by two more pragmatic concerns. First, it seems that the community realizes that forcing any such return would be regarded by the unrepentant "returnees" to be a return to what was or would become for them a prison. Prisoners make very bad covenant members. Second, it is likely that such an unwilling and resentful presence in the community would have a very bad effect on other members of the community, especially younger members who are still unsure of their own religious convictions and who might try to emulate these "captives" as part of some sort of adolescent rebellion.

Finally, this *de facto* recognition of the right of religious liberty, even for apostates, should also be understood as theologically *de jure*. For, even though the covenant originates in God's free choice to elect His people, nonetheless, the practical efficacy of the covenant depends on the free choice of the people to confirm their election, both collectively and individually. Indeed, God's covenant with the Jewish people is expressly framed as beginning with God's free choice but as depending on their free response to become operative. "I call heaven and earth to witness against you this day, that I have set before thee life and death, the blessing and the curse; *therefore choose life*, that thou mayest live, thou and thy seed" (Deuteronomy 30:19).

A Christian Case for Religious Freedom, by Nicholas Wolterstorff

In the Christian tradition there have been three major lines of argument for the civil right to religious freedom.

The oldest and most common line of argument is that God has no interest in coerced worship; what God desires of His human creatures is that they worship Him freely. One finds this line of thought already in the early church father Lactantius: "nothing is so much a matter of free will as religion." This has often been elaborated by appealing to a certain understanding of what makes worship authentic. To quote Lactantius again:

> The worship of God . . . requires full commitment (*maximam devotionem*) and faith. For how will God love the worshipper if He Himself is not loved by him, or grant to the petitioner whatever he asks when he draws near and offers his prayer without sincerity (*ex animo*) or reverence. But they [the pagans], when they come to offer sacrifice, offer to their gods nothing from within, nothing of themselves, no innocence of mind, no reverence, no awe.[42]

Because authentic worship requires sincerity, it cannot be coerced. People can, of course, be coerced into performing one or another religious practice; they can be coerced into kneeling and saying certain words. But for one's worship of God to be authentic it must be expressive of one's love or one's "awe" and one's "reverence," as Lactantius says. Without these, one is simply going through the motions. This understanding of authentic worship reflects Jesus' critique of the piety of the

Pharisees of his day; and this reflects, in turn, the critique by the Old Testament prophets of the piety of their day.

A second line of argument, employing the idea of natural rights and natural duties, emerged most clearly in the early modern period in Western Europe and America and was given memorable expression in the constitutions composed by the new American states in the 1770s. But it, too, was probably already anticipated by the Church Fathers. According to Tertullian in the second century, "It is a human law and a natural right (*naturalis potestatis*) that one should worship whatever he intends (*quod putaverit colere*); the religious practice of one person neither harms nor helps another. It is no part of religion to coerce religious practice, for it is by free choice not coercion that we should be led to religion (*nec religionis est cogere religionem, quae sponte suscipi debeat, non vi*)."[43]

On this line of argument, everyone has the natural right or duty to worship God according to the dictates of his own conscience; accordingly, everyone should have the civil right to be free to do so. The Pennsylvania Constitution of 1776 puts it thus: "All men have a natural and inalienable right to worship Almighty God according to the dictates of their own conscience and understanding. And . . . no man ought or of right can be compelled to attend any religious worship . . . contrary to or against his own free will and consent." The Maryland Constitution of 1776 speaks of duty rather than right: "It is the duty of every man to worship God in such manner as he thinks most acceptable to him."

A third line of argument grounds the civil right to religious freedom in the dignity of the human person; to deprive a person of religious freedom is to violate that person's dignity. The declaration on religious freedom issued by Vatican II, *Dignitatis Humanae*, argued in this way: "the right to religious freedom is based on the very dignity of the human person, . . . not in the subjective attitude of the individual but in his very nature."

Each of these arguments employs a certain principle to reach its conclusion: a principle concerning the authenticity of worship, concerning our natural rights and duties, or concerning our dignity as human persons.

In a recent writing of mine I have advanced a fourth line of argument, one that concerns the nature and existence of the Christian church.[44] The church is born of the spirit, not of the flesh. And always, when it emerges in some society, some members of that society willingly join and others do not. Thus wherever the church emerges it either produces a religious fissure in that society or increases the fissure that was already there. Some Slavs join; others do not. Some French join; others do not. Some Americans join; others do not. Thus the church is not Slavic, nor is it French, nor is it American.

What follows, given that the church is born not of the flesh but of the spirit, is that wherever it emerges, the church will struggle for the freedom of its members to worship God in Christ and will resist all efforts to coerce those who decline to worship God in Christ to go through the motions of doing so. And justice requires that the freedom the church asks for itself it will ask for others as well.

Altogether, then, here are four Christian lines of argument for religious freedom. In the first and last, the theological content of the argument is explicit; in the second and third, it is more implicit. Each of these lines of argument has been elaborated in detail; here I have excised all details and presented just the core idea.

An Islamic Case for Religious Freedom, by Abdullah Saeed

Whether people have the right to freedom of belief and religion is a somewhat difficult issue to address from an "Islamic" perspective. Although the Qur'an and the practice of Prophet Muhammad, the two most important sources of Islamic norms and law, are supportive of the right to freedom of belief and religion, classical Islamic legal scholarship takes a somewhat different view. It restricted certain aspects of the religious liberty of Muslims and non-Muslims, despite the liberty the Qur'an gave to both non-Muslims and Muslims to choose their beliefs and manifest their religions. For non-Muslims, the most significant limitation imposed by classical Islamic law was to constrain some areas of their public expression of religion, although it allowed them to retain their own religions and be governed by their religious norms. For Muslims, classical Islamic law stipulated the death penalty for those who left Islam. These restrictions emerged in Muslim tradition for a variety of political and social reasons but in reality they have little support from the Qur'an and the practice of Prophet Muhammad.[45] In the modern period, Muslim arguments for religious liberty are often based on an analysis of what these two sources (and in particular the Qur'an) have to say on the issue of religious liberty.[46] Increasingly Muslim thinkers today are using the arguments found in the Qur'an to defend religious liberty from an Islamic perspective.

Broadly, the Qur'an views religion, as proclaimed by God's messengers, as a human good (Q 17:15). For the Qur'an, belief in the One God, the Creator and Sustainer, is the basis for religion and morality, and it maintains that people should protect this belief assiduously. One of the most important functions of a government is therefore to protect the right to believe in the One God, without pressure from anyone, including prophets.[47]

Although religion and belief in the One God is a human good, the Qur'an does not expect all people to follow this path.[48] It leaves people with considerable leeway to reject this belief and religion and to follow their own desires (Q 18:29). God provided people with free will and choice at the very beginning when creating Adam and Eve. God then tested them. In making their own choice Adam and Eve failed this original test, but their failure did not lead to the eternal damnation of the entire human race.

The Qur'an presents this testing of free will as part of God's plan for humankind.[49] An essential part of this testing therefore concerns the freedom to choose whether to believe in the One God.

We are responsible for what we do and fail to do on earth, including believing in the One God and following His commandments and ethical-moral code. While the Qur'an grants us the freedom to believe or not to believe, it associates this choice with weighty consequences. God will hold each of us accountable on the Day of Judgment for the choices we make during our lifetime, when we will stand before Him and answer for what we did or failed to do. As with belief, this means that salvation is an individual effort, not a collective one; the Qur'an does not present the question of belief fundamentally as a collective matter.[50]

Theologically, the Qur'an sees every human being as God's perfect creation, blessed with intellect and free will. It teaches that God gave humankind the intellect and ability to discern right and wrong.[51] All of these notions are strongly compatible with the idea of religious liberty.

A great many Qur'anic verses specify without ambiguity that the question of faith and belief is a personal matter between each individual and God. The Qur'an teaches that we have the ability to consider the options for ourselves and the freedom to make the decision whether to believe in God (for instance, Q 17:15). It proclaims, for example, "Let him who wills believe in it [Islam], and let him who wills, reject it" (Q 18:29) and "Whoever chooses to follow the right path, follows it for his own good; and if anyone wills to go astray, say [O Prophet, to him] 'I am only a warner'" (Q 6:104).

One of the most crucial ways that the Qur'an affirms each person's autonomy and freedom to choose is by condemning the use of coercion in matters of faith. "There shall be no coercion in matters of faith. Distinct has now become the right way from [the way of] error: hence, he who rejects the powers of evil and believes in God has indeed taken hold of a support most unfailing, which shall never give way: for God is all-hearing, all-knowing" (Q 2: 256).[52] The Qur'an considers forced belief to be totally unacceptable because it is only through genuine conviction and belief that a person can truly come to Islam. It encourages Muslims to invite others to Islam "in the way that is best" (Q 29:46), using courteous advice, sound reasoning, and elegant persuasion rather than force.[53]

The Qur'an states that the Prophet Muhammad's role was simply to show people "the true path" and not to compel them to believe (Q 3:20). It says that Prophet Muhammad's duty was only to convey the message of Islam (Q 24:54; 5:99), and his actual practice suggests that he supported this idea of free choice regarding religious belief.

However, any discussion of religious liberty in Islam must address the issue of apostasy and the prescription of classical Islamic law that it be punished by death. For Muslims, this is perhaps the most problematic restriction when it comes to religious liberty, but it is one that has little support from Islam's two most important primary sources. While conversion from Islam (apostasy) is considered a great sin, one that has weighty consequences in the life after death, the Qur'an does not specify any kind of worldly punishment for apostasy, let alone death.[54]

Moreover, there is no indication that the Prophet Muhammad ever imposed the death penalty on anyone for the simple act of conversion from Islam.[55] On the contrary, one hadith in the collection of Bukhari (one of the most important and reliable collections of hadith for Sunni Muslims) describes a man who came to Medina and converted to Islam. Shortly after his arrival he decided that he wanted to go back to his former religion and asked the Prophet for permission to do so. The Prophet let him go free without imposing the death penalty or any other punishment.[56]

When it comes to perhaps the most important saying attributed to the Prophet about the death penalty for apostasy—the hadith, "Whoever changes his religion, kill him"—there are specific concerns about taking it at face value. Apart from some questions about the authenticity of the hadith, there are concerns about its content, as it is notably brief and general. Taking this hadith literally, it could mean that the death penalty applies even to those who convert to Islam.[57] Interpretation therefore will have to decide its practical meaning. More importantly, at the time of the Prophet Muhammad, conversion from Islam would have meant rejection of the Muslim community and joining their non-Muslim opponents, and taking up arms against the Muslim community. Thus the punishment is perhaps not for a simple act of conversion but for the equivalent of "treason."[58]

Overall, the evidence from Islam's two primary sources is that faith must be based on personal conviction, not coercion. Individuals should be free to believe or not to believe in God or in a religion as part of their exercise of the freedom God bestows on all human beings.

CHAPTER FIVE

A Legal Case for Religious Freedom

*Religion is unlike other human activities, or at least the [American]
founders thought so. The proper relation between religion and government
was a subject of great debate in the founding generation, and the
[United States] Constitution includes two clauses that apply to religion and
do not apply to anything else. This debate and these clauses
presuppose that religion is in some way a special human activity,
requiring special rules applicable only to it.*

—DOUGLAS LAYCOCK, PROFESSOR OF LAW,
UNIVERSITY OF VIRGINIA

If religious freedom protects natural human inclinations to understand a transcendent order; if it is positively associated with other freedoms, as well as social, political, and economic goods such as order, stability, and prosperity; if a compelling case can be made for it on grounds of moral philosophy; if it draws sustenance from the taproots of theology itself—how then can we, in practice, protect religious freedom, safeguarding the space people need to explore and express the truth about a divine order for themselves, as individuals and faith communities?

We can begin by turning to the same safeguard on which we rely for freedoms of every kind: the rule of law. Religious freedom in both its negative and positive dimensions enjoys an honored place in the law of the United States, of numerous countries around the world, and of the international community. But how secure is the position of religious freedom in these various jurisdictions? The relevant constitutions, legal codes, and international covenants give us good reason to believe that religious freedom warrants and receives special attention and respect. But its position may be more precarious than these appearances suggest.

A growing number of legal thinkers, and legal judgments, treat religious freedom with suspicion if not downright disrespect. Warning of this trend, John Finnis has remarked, "some contemporary American legal and constitutional theorists hold that there is nothing about religion or its free exercise that calls for particular respect, or any mention in constitutional bills of rights."[59] Finnis particularly criticizes constitutional scholars Christopher Eisgruber and Lawrence Sager, who have argued that "[w]e need to abandon the idea that it is the unique value of religious practices that sometimes entitles them to constitutional attention."[60]

University of Chicago law professor Brian Leiter is an even more forceful and radical example of the skeptical school. He raises the question in the most basic terms: "[W]hy tolerate religion?" His answer: "Not because of anything that has to do with it being religion as such." Or as he elaborates: "[T]here is no principled reason for legal or constitutional regimes to *single out* religion for protection; there is no moral or epistemic consideration that favors special legal solicitude towards beliefs that conjoin *categorical commands* with *insulation from evidence*."[61] As is apparent from Leiter's prejudicial definition of religious beliefs as "categorical commands" conjoined with "insulation from evidence," religion is so far from deserving special protection that it deserves special distrust and suspicion. At best, religious freedom should be considered just a subset of a wider freedom of conscience or right to autonomy that has nothing to do with truth, religion, or the pursuit of an unseen order of reality.

But the law of the United States and of numerous other societies presupposes that religion is special. Michael W. McConnell puts the point memorably:

> Religion is a special phenomenon, in part, because it plays such a wide variety of roles in human life: it is an institution, but it is more than that; it is an ideology or worldview, but it is more than that; it is a set of personal loyalties and locus of community, akin to family ties, but it is more than that; it is an aspect of identity, but it is more than that; it provides answers to questions of ultimate reality, and offers a connection to the transcendent; but it is more than that. Religion cannot be reduced to a subset of any larger category.[62]

The United States Constitution, of course, did not originally contain the familiar language of the First Amendment, declaring that "Congress shall make no law respecting an establishment of religion, or prohibiting the free exercise thereof." This language, like the rest of what is called the Bill of Rights, was proposed by the First Congress in 1789, and ratified by the states over the next two years, in response to concerns that the new Constitution lacked sufficient protections for various freedoms in its original provisions. When these concerns were met, as President George Washington later assured the Jewish congregation of Newport, Rhode Island, the United States would be devoted to more than mere "toleration" of less powerful religious groups by more powerful ones. It would instead protect their "inherent natural rights" and give "to bigotry no sanction, to persecution no assistance."[63]

Bills of rights were familiar devices by 1787, and the framers of the original Constitution were devoted to religious freedom. So it is worth considering why they did not include a provision like the future First Amendment from the beginning. One part of the answer is that the original Constitution did at least (in Article VI) prohibit any "religious Test" to serve in federal office, opening up public service to the nation to any citizen whose merit recommended him to voters or to elected officials making appointments to office, and making mere sectarian prejudice appear discreditable as a motive force in voting. A fuller answer is suggested in the argument of James Madison (who was at first resistant to amendments but later led the effort to add them) in the *Federalist* No. 51:

> In a free government, the security for civil rights must be the same as that for religious rights. It consists in the one case in the multiplicity of interests, and in the other, in the multiplicity of sects. . . . In the extended republic of the United States, and among the great variety of interests, parties and sects which it embraces, a coalition of a majority of the whole society could seldom take place on any other principles than those of justice and the general good.[64]

Religion thus figured in the "new political science" of the American founders. Just as social, political, and economic diversity would have a salutary effect in a large-scale republic—where a great variety of interests would find it to their advantage to compromise—so too religious diversity would itself contribute to religious freedom, as no religious sect would be in a position to effect, or even be seriously tempted to try, an outright suppression of competing sects or faiths.

Undergirding this political science of liberty—and forming the common understanding of *religious* freedom particularly in the American founding—was a clear view of the limits of political authority. Gerard Bradley has described this understanding succinctly:

> The Founders' most important insight into religious liberty as a civil right was to see that the truth about sectarian matters—sacred doctrine, modes of worship, forms of church polity, rules for church membership in good standing—could be kept out of political life.[65]

The political order, in this view, simply lacked *jurisdiction* over questions that properly belong to religious faith and to religious communities. This was the principle that the founders sought to install in the clause of the First Amendment now often said to be *two* clauses, concerning "establishment" and "free exercise" of religion.

This did not mean that the framers of the American Constitution were "secularists" in the way that expression is commonly used today, to describe political actors who seek to chase religion from public life and "privatize" it (perhaps in hopes of its quietly dying out). In fact, what Bradley calls the "privatization project" in modern American constitutional law is largely owing to ill-considered decisions of the U.S. Supreme Court concerning the First Amendment over the last six decades or so. In many respects the Court's tortuous path through the law of religious freedom has not been good for either religion *or* the political order, on any reasonable understanding.

But this essay is not the place to try untangling the mare's nest of First Amendment religion jurisprudence. What we can say, while scholars, activists, and jurists continue to struggle over the proper shape and boundaries of religious freedom in constitutional law, is that the American experiment in providing maximum political space for the religious yearnings of the human heart has been, on balance, a great success story. This success can be traced to the fact that the American founders did not agree with our modern-day skeptics about the status of religious freedom. It was not, for them, simply a particular but mundane case of some more general freedom of thought, or freedom of association. Religious freedom rested on its own bottom, distinctive in its own right because, as James Madison put it in a passage we have already quoted, it sprang from human obligations to the more-than-human that are "precedent, both in order of time and in degree of obligation, to the claims of Civil Society."

Global Recognition that Religion Is Distinctive

Since the founding of the United States, the overwhelming global trend has been to treat religion and religious freedom in just this way elsewhere too: as an aspect of our humanity, and a liberty, that have a special character and special dignity. Consider just one example, though a particularly significant one: the constitution of the Republic of India.

When the Constituent Assembly of India designed its constitution, it engaged in extensive public debate about what special protections, if any, it should provide the country's citizens with respect to religion. The Assembly concluded that the constitution should devote a special article to the "Right to Freedom of Religion," and that this right should be defined in expansive terms: "all persons are equally entitled to freedom of conscience and the right freely to profess, practise [*sic*] and propagate religion."

The Assembly also judged that the constitution should afford religious life what can best be described as an independent and respected space.

> Subject to public order, morality and health, every religious denom-
> ination or any section thereof shall have the right—(*a*) to establish

and maintain institutions for religious and charitable purposes; (*b*) to manage its own affairs in matters of religion; (*c*) to own and acquire movable and immovable property; and (*d*) to administer such property in accordance with law.

India, therefore, lives under a constitution that formally respects religious freedom in all its dimensions.

Gathering in the immediate aftermath of World War II, the international community affirmed the universal right of religious freedom. As Mary Ann Glendon observes, the Lebanese Christian diplomat Charles Malik, spearheading the work of the UN's Human Rights Commission in 1947,

> proposed four principles to guide the work of the Commission: First, the human person is more important than any national or cultural group to which he may belong. Second, a person's mind and conscience are his most sacred and inviolable possessions. Third, any pressure from the state, church, or any other group aimed at coercing consent is unacceptable. Fourth, since groups, as well as individuals, may be right or wrong, each person's freedom of conscience must be supreme.

Malik, Glendon goes on to point out, eschewed any form of facile modern individualism:

> The person, as Malik used that term, was neither Marx's "species being" nor the lone rights-bearer imagined by many Anglo-American thinkers. Without derogating from the unique value of each human being, Malik saw the human person as constituted in important ways by and through his relationships—with his family, his community, his nation, and his God.[66]

Adopted by the United Nations General Assembly on December 10, 1948, by a vote of 48 to 0, with eight abstentions, the Universal Declaration of Human Rights affirmed:

> Everyone has the right to freedom of thought, conscience and religion; this right includes freedom to change his religion or belief, and freedom, either alone or in community with others and in public or private, to manifest his religion or belief in teaching, practice, worship and observance. (Article 18)

Religious freedom, the Universal Declaration says, is a universal right. It belongs to every person. It includes the interior or "private" right to believe in accordance with one's own conscience as well as the exterior or "public" right to manifest one's religion in "teaching, practice, worship and observance." It is a right that all persons must have the freedom to express as individuals ("alone") and with others ("in community").

If anything, these principles have come to be affirmed with even greater clarity in the more than sixty years since 1948, and by an even larger proportion of the international community. The International Covenant on Civil and Political Rights, adopted by the UN General Assembly in 1966, and as of 2010 signed or ratified (or both) by the vast majority of the world's states, reaffirmed Article 18 of the Universal Declaration but went even further, adding that "[n]o one shall be subject to coercion which would impair his freedom to have or to adopt a religion or belief of his choice." And thirty years ago, the United Nations General Assembly devoted special attention to religious freedom's importance when, after years of internal study and debate, it issued a "Declaration on the Elimination of All Forms of Intolerance and of Discrimination Based on Religion or Belief" on November 25, 1981.

Building on previous international statements, the 1981 Declaration insists that no one shall be subject to religious intolerance or discrimination "by any State, institution, group of persons, or person on grounds of religion or other beliefs," with religious intolerance and discrimination defined as "any distinction, exclusion, restriction or preference based on religion or belief and having as its purpose or as its effect nullification or impairment of the recognition, enjoyment or exercise of human rights and fundamental freedoms on an equal basis." Such discrimination "constitutes an affront to human dignity and a disavowal of the principles of the Charter of the United Nations, and shall be condemned as a violation of the human rights and fundamental freedoms proclaimed in the Universal Declaration of Human Rights."

The 1981 Declaration on Intolerance went on to elaborate that religious freedom generates a host of specific rights, including the right of parents or legal guardians "to organize the life within the family in accordance with their religion or belief"; the right to establish humanitarian institutions; the right to disseminate relevant publications; the right to teach a religion or belief; the right to train, appoint, elect or designate appropriate leaders "called for by the requirements and standards of any religion or belief"; and the right to establish and maintain communications with individuals and communities in matters of religion and belief at the national and international levels. Significantly, too, the 1981 Declaration led to the appointment of a United Nations Special Rapporteur on freedom of religion or belief in 1986.

Emphatically and repeatedly, then, the international community has singled out a package of rights and freedoms associated with religion for special attention and protection. These rights and freedoms are so important that they are to be limited only when "necessary to protect public safety, order, health, or morals or the fundamental rights and freedoms of others" (International Covenant on Civil and Political Rights, Article 18, paragraph 3).

Beyond international statements and covenants, the overwhelming majority of the world's countries affirm a commitment to religious freedom in their own laws and constitutions. In fact, 83 percent of countries with a population of at least two million offer constitutional guarantees of religious freedom, and another 8 percent provide legal guarantees of religious freedom. Only 9 percent—thirteen countries—fail formally to acknowledge what has been increasingly recognized as a universal right.[67]

Law and Reality

The status of national and international law seems to bode well for the rights of religious individuals and communities around the world. One might come away complacent and optimistic from a survey of the legal landscape alone. Many legal codes appear to acknowledge that religion and religious freedom are uniquely valuable, both to individuals and to states.[68]

But the gap between law and reality is, unfortunately, a stark one, and not just in the United States. Notwithstanding solemn undertakings in legal codes, protection of religious freedom by governments is eroding worldwide. As we have noted, scores of millions of people are subject to severe restrictions on their religious freedom, many of them suffering violent religious persecution.

It appears, then, that the establishment of legal norms is a necessary but insufficient bulwark against the abuse of human beings because of their religious beliefs and practices. The result is a humanitarian crisis of the first order. But the erosion of religious liberty has also created a crisis of international security, albeit one that is rarely remarked in the United States or elsewhere. It is to the strategic dimensions of that problem that we now turn. What, if anything, can the nations of the world do to reduce religious persecution and advance religious freedom? And why should they make the effort?

PART TWO

Religious Freedom and International Affairs

CHAPTER SIX

The Strategic Case for Religious Freedom

*In the future days, which we seek to make secure, we look forward
to a world founded upon four essential human freedoms.
The first is freedom of speech and expression. . . . The second is freedom
of every person to worship God in his own way. . . . The third is freedom from
want. . . . The fourth is freedom from fear, which, translated into world
terms, means . . . that no nation will be in a position to commit an act
of physical aggression against any neighbor. . . . That is no vision of a
distant millennium. It is a definite basis for a kind of world
attainable in our own time and generation.*

—PRESIDENT FRANKLIN DELANO ROOSEVELT,
"FOUR FREEDOMS SPEECH," JANUARY 1941

The basis for a secure future is freedom. That is how President Roosevelt saw it in his famous "Four Freedoms Speech" in 1941, just as the world was descending into total war.[69]

Among the four freedoms President Roosevelt singled out as the essential building blocks of global security was religious freedom.

Roosevelt's linkage of global security with fundamental freedoms reminds us that there has long been a connection between how a nation treats its own citizens and how it acts in the world. And how it treats its religious citizens is of particular importance. Neither the pacifists who opposed the war, nor the realists who supported it, fully understood this point.

The record of the Nazi and Stalinist regimes—not incidentally joined together in a non-aggression pact at the very moment Roosevelt gave his "Four Freedoms" speech—highlighted just how unrealistic both pacifism and realism were. Neither possessed the moral vision to foresee the threat posed by regimes that, in pursuit of radical ideological goals, wantonly destroyed their own peoples and then turned outward against the world. Both Nazi Germany and the Soviet imperium demonstrated that there could be no lasting global security when powerful regimes flout the most basic of human rights.

After the war Franklin Roosevelt's widow Eleanor, and the Lebanese statesman Charles Malik, led the effort to draft the Universal Declaration of Human Rights. Mrs. Roosevelt was convinced that the world would not become more peaceful and secure until it became more just and free. As it had been in her husband's vision, religious freedom was singled out as an essential foundation of a more secure world. Article 18 of the Universal Declaration insists that "*[e]veryone* has the right to freedom of thought, conscience and religion."[70]

This was something genuinely new in human affairs. The world was beginning to acknowledge for the first time that religious freedom demands respect not only because of the dignity and worth of individual human beings, but also because of the need for global security and stability. If the world's nations seek to advance human dignity *and* security and stability, they must also advance religious liberty. To put it in realist terms, it is in their vital interest to do so.

In short, a kind of "religious realism" was beginning to assert itself in the discourse of international affairs.

In recent years several nations have recognized the interconnection of religious freedom, their own national interests, and the interests of international peace and security. In 1998 the U.S. Congress mandated the advancement of religious freedom in U.S. foreign policy by passing the International Religious Freedom Act (IRFA), which President Bill Clinton signed into law. IRFA established an Office of International Religious Freedom within the State Department and an independent Commission to monitor the Department and issue its own recommendations.[71]

In 2006 the National Security Strategy (NSS) of the United States formally incorporated the promotion of religious freedom as a national security imperative, one that could help democracy take root and, at the same time, undermine religion-based terrorism:

> Effective democracies . . . [h]onor and uphold basic human rights, including freedom of religion, conscience, speech, assembly, association, and press . . . and . . . [l]imit the reach of government, protecting the institutions of civil society, including the family, religious communities, voluntary associations, private property, independent business, and a market economy. . . . In effective democracies, freedom is indivisible. Political, religious, and economic liberty advance together and reinforce each other. . . . The advance of freedom and human dignity through democracy is the long-term solution to the transnational terrorism of today.[72]

If democracy is to be lasting and stable, yielding benefits to its citizens and its neighbors, it must be grounded in an interlocking web of fundamental freedoms, including religious freedom. None is sufficient alone, and each is necessary to the whole. Accordingly, when religious freedom is absent—as is often the case in the twenty-first century—democracy cannot take root.

Just as importantly—for American security and international security—when there is no democracy, or when democracy is fragile and weak, religion-related terrorism is far more likely to be incubated, nourished, and exported around the world. That is true because religious actors are less likely to turn to violence when they are participants in a liberal democratic system. Liberal democracy encourages their ideas, but also subjects them to liberal norms and limits, including the foundational principle of equality under the law. And democracy requires religious actors who wish to influence public policy to submit their beliefs to public scrutiny, subjecting them to criticism and debate from other views, both secular and religious.

Other nations are turning their attention to this argument and giving religious freedom more prominence in their foreign policies. In 2004, for example, Canada's Parliamentary Subcommittee on Human Rights and International Development adopted a resolution urging the government "to make the protection and promotion of the right to freedom of religion and belief a central element of its efforts to defend human rights internationally." In 2011, Canadian Prime Minister Stephen Harper announced the establishment of an Office of International Religious Freedom. That same year, the Foreign and Commonwealth office of the United Kingdom held a conference on religious freedom and foreign policy, and German Chancellor Angela Merkel expressed a desire for greater attention to the issue. The European Union has taken several high-profile steps to promote global religious freedom more effectively.[73]

All these individuals and nations are on to something. Religious freedom is indeed an essential means of parrying a wide range of strategic threats to global security and to the interests of free nations.

Strategic Arguments for Religious Freedom

In what follows, we articulate the strategic case for religious freedom. We argue that religious repression and religious freedom are closely related to some of the major strategic challenges faced by all nations of the world, especially those aspiring to peace, security, and freedom. While we acknowledge that many religious traditions have produced violent extremists, we believe that in the twenty-first century Islamist extremism and terrorism pose one of the gravest threats to peace, security, and freedom. We argue that religious repression is one cause of this deadly phenomenon. Repression has helped incubate those Islamist ideologies and movements that endanger democracy and global security, and are a leading cause of national, regional, and global instability.

By the same token, we contend that liberal democratic political orders grounded in religious freedom can weaken the appeal of, and increase the competitive alternatives to, religious radicalism. If religious repression radicalizes and desta-bilizes, religious freedom counter-radicalizes and stabilizes. Religious freedom should therefore be an essential ingredient in any effective long-term strategy for weakening radical religious movements and reducing the dynamics of violence and instability that pose a serious threat to global security and national interests.

In what follows we employ American interests as a touchstone in our analysis, with particular policy proposals for the United States, informed by over a decade of American diplomatic experience in the field of international religious freedom. However, we believe the analysis that follows is not exclusive to the United States. It can and should be applied to any nation that seeks to advance human dignity and ordered liberty, as well as international peace, stability, and security. Our rec-ommendations are adaptable by any nation seeking to advance religious freedom.

Defining Strategic Interests and the Major Threats to Those Interests

Consider America's strategic interests, which are similar to the interests of many nations. America seeks a world in which neither governments nor violent movements threaten its citizens, homeland, property, or vital interests abroad. It seeks a world of trading partners and economic growth (for itself and others), of security grounded in ordered liberty, of human rights and social stability. It seeks to maintain the capabilities to defend itself, to maintain alliances, and to pursue its objectives through bilateral and multilateral diplomacy.

Now consider how international religious freedom might further those interests, in particular by helping advance security through the establishment of stable democracies, and by helping the United States defend its homeland and citizens against violent religion-based extremism and terrorism.

Who and what constitute the most lethal enemies? They are not metaphorical—a set of vague "challenges" or faceless "dangers." At this moment, specific persons and groups strive to kill innocent people, attack the citizens and property of the United States and many other nations, overthrow regimes friendly to these nations, and impose an oppressive vision on whole societies. And if these enemies were to acquire the destructive capability they ardently seek, they would pose a direct threat to the United States and free peoples everywhere.

"Terrorists" and "terrorism" are the labels we often apply to these enemies. But these are taxonomic categories, not enemies; they name a genus that contains widely disparate phenomena, some of which bear little relevance and certainly pose no threat to the United States or to international security.

That a more specific enemy poses a more specific threat to America was articulated with searing clarity by the bipartisan "9/11 Commission Report" in 2004:

> [T]he enemy is not just "terrorism," some generic evil. This vagueness blurs the strategy. The catastrophic threat at this moment in history is

> more specific. It is the threat posed by *Islamist* terrorism—especially
> the al Qaeda network, its affiliates, and its ideology. . . . Usama Bin
> Ladin and other Islamist terrorist leaders draw on a long tradition
> of extreme intolerance within one stream of Islam (a minority tra-
> dition), from at least Ibn Taimiyyah, through the founders of Wah-
> habism, through the Muslim Brotherhood, to Sayyid Qutb. That
> stream is motivated by religion and does not distinguish politics from
> religion, thus distorting both. . . . Bin Ladin and Islamist terrorists
> mean exactly what they say: to them America is the font of all evil,
> the "head of the snake."[74]

The particular enemy America faces is Islamist terrorism—a stream of violent
intolerance "motivated by religion." This form of terrorism is distinctive in that it
is both deeply religious, and "does not distinguish politics from religion," in a way
that does not admit religious freedom.

How did this threat emerge? Why have so many Muslim-majority countries
witnessed the rise of movements that advance their ideas and redress their
grievances through violence? Why have so many Muslim-majority countries seen
the formation of groups and parties that seek to impose their theological visions
through quasi-totalitarian systems of law and politics?

Why have so many Muslim-majority nations that are struggling to embrace
democracy so far failed to contain, let alone eliminate, the lethal ideas of radical
Islamism? Why have they failed to retrieve and elevate earlier Islamic teachings—
for example, those of the rationalist schools—that might form the basis for a
modern Islamic commitment to human rights and religious freedom?[75]

As the 9/11 Commission notes, the answer to these questions begins with the
survival and flourishing of a particular tradition of radical ideas. Muslim thinkers
from Ibn Tamiyyah to Sayyid Qutb have developed political theologies that make
violent, intolerant politics a theological obligation. The malignant effects of these
ideas are fed by stated grievances against the United States and its foreign policy.

There are two broad global trends that put in context the survival and expansion
of violent, extremist interpretations of Islam.

The first trend is what some scholars have called the "global political resurgence
of religion"—a worldwide increase in political ambition and activism on the part of
virtually all major religious communities. This pattern is not confined to Muslim-
majority nations, but it certainly includes them. From the events in Iran that
swept the Shah of Iran from power in the late 1970s to the events in Egypt today,
Islamic groups of all kinds throughout the Muslim-majority world are rising up
to influence public life and reshape societies. Some have been liberal and modern,
others violent and extreme.

The second trend is continuing and increasing repression of religious activities
in most Muslim-majority countries. In some, governments actively repress all
religious groups. In others, governments favor—yet also typically control and

manipulate—one religious group while repressing others. This trend is unsurprising when it appears in theocratic regimes such as Saudi Arabia, Sudan, and Iran. But it has also emerged in Muslim-majority countries with nascent democracies such as Pakistan, Iraq, Afghanistan, Indonesia, Turkey, and Egypt.

Whether we are speaking of authoritarian nations or democracies, religious resurgence *and* repression have been on a decades-long collision course in the vast arc of Muslim-majority countries from Nigeria and Morocco to Afghanistan and Indonesia. As religious groups have intensified their efforts to emerge, their governments have intensified their efforts to repress and control them.

In only a few other parts of the world—notably Communist countries such as China and Vietnam, and post-Communist nations such as Russia—is the clash between rising religion and repressive government as sustained and severe.[76] It is true that restrictions on religious liberty have also been increasing in Europe. But while those restrictions have not, for the most part, resulted in persecution, they may have exacerbated violent tendencies in some Islamist movements.[77] In Latin America and other parts of the world, thanks in part to political democratization and liberalization, the trend has been less government repression and more political openness, including openness and freedom for religious groups.[78]

But in the Muslim-majority world of struggling democracies and authoritarian regimes, resurgence and repression have met like tectonic plates violently pushing against each other. Two momentous consequences have been the failure of democracy to take root, and the spread of organized Islamist extremism and terrorism.

In order to grasp the strategic threat of religious repression and the strategic necessity of encouraging the growth of Muslim democracies grounded in religious freedom, let us briefly explore the worldwide political resurgence of religion, and the particular nature of its resurgence in the lands of Islam.

Religion's Pervasive Resurgence[79]

"Is God Dead?" a *Time* magazine cover story asked on April 8, 1966. The mid-1960s may have marked the apogee of secularism's dominance over modern world affairs. The conventional wisdom shared by many intellectual and political elites the world over was that modernization would inevitably extinguish religion's vitality. With ever-expanding material security and education, fewer people would turn to religion either for comfort or knowledge, and its power—above all, its *public* power—would inevitably diminish to the vanishing point. In 1968, the eminent British historian Arnold Toynbee represented this consensus when he wrote with breathtaking sweep and confidence that "*all* current religions . . . have been losing their hold on the hearts and consciences and minds of their former adherents."[80]

When Toynbee wrote those words, however, global politics was already beginning to pivot. If 1966 was the zenith of secularism's global self-confidence, 1967 marked the beginning of the end of its global hegemony. In that year, the leader of secular Arab nationalism, Gamal Abdel Nasser, suffered a humiliating defeat at the hands of the Israeli Army during the Six-Day War. From that point onward, the legitimacy of Nasserite Arab nationalism suffered a precipitous decline. By the end of the 1970s, hardly more than ten years after *Time*'s "death of God" cover, Iran's Ayatollah Khomeini, "born again" U.S. President Jimmy Carter, and Pope John Paul II had dramatically demonstrated the increasing political strength of religious movements and their leaders.

Ten years later, a combination of rosary-wielding Solidarity workers in Poland and Kalashnikov-wielding *mujahideen* in Afghanistan had helped defeat atheistic Soviet Communism. Such developments led French political scientist Gilles Kepel to observe that it was more accurate to talk about the "revenge of God" than the death of God.[81] Then, just after the turn of the century, nineteen hijackers transformed world politics and the strategic priorities of the United States by crashing passenger jets into the World Trade Center, the Pentagon, and a rural Pennsylvania field, crying "God is great" as they did so.

In sum, reports of God's demise have been greatly exaggerated. We now live in an era when, for better or for worse, religion is a robust global force. Whether in the form of Islamist radicalism, evangelical Protestantism, Hindu nationalism, Eastern Orthodox nationalism, Roman Catholic evangelicalism, Buddhist revivalism, or Jewish Zionism, religion is increasingly vibrant, assertive, and politicized the world over.

What is the explanation for this remarkable phenomenon? Some have suggested that religion's intense political activity in the modern world is best interpreted as a sign of embattlement, weakness, and decline. If religion's position and influence were really secure, as it was in pre-modern traditional societies, it would not need to resort to extraordinary political means to advance its influence, or so the argument goes. "[Religious actors] and their devout followers fight back in their own ways against the spreading vulgarization and secularization of societies that seem tempted to dispense with religion altogether," wrote *Washington Post* columnist Jim Hoagland in 2006. "These are by and large counterrevolutionary movements, out of step with a secularizing march by history that many of them would destroy rather than accept."[82]

In fact, global religion shows little sign of declining in the face of modernization or any "secularizing march by history." Most objective measures demonstrate that the period in which economic and political modernization has been most intense and globally expansive—i.e. the last thirty to forty years—has witnessed a parallel increase in religious vitality. The latter, along with global declines in secular ideologies and movements and the global expansion of democracy, has been a major driver of the resurgence in religious politics.

It is also true that signs of religious renewal and politicization have been less robust in some parts of the world, particularly Europe. But Europe, along with relatively sparsely populated European settler societies such as Canada, Australia, and New Zealand, is clearly the secular exception to the global rule of religious vitality.

Beyond Europe, the world's major religious communities have not only expanded and religious commitment intensified, but religion has also become more public and political. This has been a particularly striking characteristic of Islamic revivalism. While secular leaders in Islamic lands, such as Egypt's Nasser or Iran's Shah, were faltering, religious beliefs, leaders, and institutions were beginning to drive political change.

The decline of Soviet communism in the 1970s and 1980s also accelerated religion's global political upsurge, including in Muslim-majority countries. The collapse of the Soviet socialist model created a political vacuum in numerous developing countries, from which religious groups, such as Islamists in the Middle East, were able to benefit. The downfall of Soviet communism also emboldened radical religious movements—above all Osama bin Laden's al Qaeda—to seek a wider field of operations, as well as to target a longer list of enemies, including the United States. The result of religion's deepening and spreading politicization is that it has become an important factor in almost every major area of world politics.

The current religious resurgence has proven so pervasive that efforts to explain it with special theories have things exactly backward. What needs special explanation is not the resurgence of religion in the last fifty years or so but the paroxysm—often violent—of secularism that swept across the world beginning with the French Revolution in 1789 and had decisively receded only by 1989. The religious revival can perhaps best be understood as an intense but natural reaction to the massive attempts to squeeze religion out of the private and, in particular, the public lives of great multitudes of humanity. While the point of departure of much analysis is that religion's public return is somehow surprising, it is perhaps more reasonable to reverse the gaze and suggest that it is the secularist expectation—in theory and in politics—that is artificial and unrealistic.

The fact of religion's global public resurgence means that the issue of religious freedom is both unavoidable and strategically important. As more and more religious actors demand social and political space, governments and societies have no choice but to confront the question of just how much freedom and influence those actors and their ideas should enjoy.

The issue of religious freedom is also strategically significant because the demand for freedom that many religious groups are articulating is insistent, urgent, and in many cases just. In virtually every part of the world religious actors increasingly seek to enjoy the right to exist, organize, and influence public opinion and political decisions on the same basis as non-religious actors. The future of numerous societies of strategic importance to the United States—including China, India, Russia, Egypt, Saudi Arabia, Pakistan, Nigeria, Afghanistan, and Iran—will depend in no small part on how they respond to the insistent demands of their diverse religious communities for freedom and security.

For our purposes, it is important to see how political Islam has evolved as part of the worldwide resurgence of religion. Unfortunately for Muslim-majority countries, their neighbors, and the world, the most influential political expressions of Islam during the last half century have tended toward violent extremism—for example, Iran's Khomeinist Shiism, Lebanon's Hezbollah, Palestinian Hamas, Egypt's Muslim Brotherhood, and, of course, al Qaeda.

It is also true—and potentially of enormous significance—that liberal democratic forms of Islamism are struggling to emerge in Muslim-majority countries, such as Turkey's ruling Justice and Development Party (AKP), or Indonesia's Nahdul Ulema, a Muslim civil society organization of some seventy million people. In part because of the impact of the latter group on Indonesian society, Freedom House has labeled Indonesia as "Free"—the only Muslim-majority nation of any size to earn that plaudit. But, as more focused studies make clear, even Indonesia and Turkey lag badly in protecting the right of religious freedom.

In retrospect, the dominant development of political Islam in Muslim-majority countries has been distinctly illiberal. While public religion was surging in a variety of guises around the globe, the radical political theologies identified in the 9/11 Report were already in place in key Muslim nations such as Saudi Arabia, Egypt, and Pakistan. From there the toxic ideas spread, sometimes clashing with nascent, liberal Islamic trends, but—because of the utter absence of religious freedom in the lands of Islam—too often winning the battle of ideas.[83]

Religion's Pervasive Repression

It is an unfortunate fact of history that a major global reaction to the worldwide resurgence of religion has been pervasive repression. Although it is occurring in a large number of nations, religious repression is especially concentrated in Muslim-majority countries, as well as in a few non–Muslim-majority countries such as China, Russia, and India.[84]

It is equally unfortunate that so little sustained attention is paid to these phenomena in the West. Some appear to think that religious repression is a minor problem, confined to a relatively small number of countries where religious groups are fanatical and invite repression, or where governments are authoritarian and inflict repression willy-nilly. Many appear to think that few people are victims of serious religious repression. Some are doubtless convinced that religious believers would be left alone if they just ratcheted down their zeal and behaved like normal people.

Human Rights Watch, which is among the world's largest and most prestigious human rights organizations, seems to represent this line of thinking. Of the approximately 325 major human rights reports it has produced since January 2008, only eight address religious repression or violations of religious freedom as a central focus. That is only a little more than 2 percent of its reporting on global human rights abuses.

In fact, by any reasonable standard, global religious repression constitutes a human rights catastrophe. As noted earlier, the nonpartisan Pew Research Center concluded in 2009 that *70 percent* of the world's population lives in countries in which restrictions on religion are severe. Tens of millions of people are subject to violent religious persecution, and, according to an update of the Pew findings in 2011, the problem is getting worse.

And yet, compared to other problems, religious repression receives little attention. It seldom assumes the form of spectacular incidents that can be captured on film or memorable statements reducible to soundbites. Occasionally it assumes dramatic form—for example, the brutal October 2010 al Qaeda attack on a Catholic Mass in Iraq, in which more than fifty people were slaughtered. But the acts by which governments and societies repress and control the religious lives of people are mostly quotidian and unspectacular, taking place well beyond the gaze of journalists and other observers.

The U.S. State Department's Annual Report on International Religious Freedom, produced every year since 1999, contains chapters on some 195 countries and is based on investigation and analysis by hundreds of American foreign service officers, official sources, and indigenous non-governmental organizations. The report notes progress on religious freedom where it is believed to have occurred but also describes abuses of religious freedom around the world in meticulous— and frequently painful—detail.

One chapter in a recent report concerned the case of Eritrea, which we highlighted in the Introduction to this essay. But the terrible truth is that depredations like those—systematic and egregious attacks on human dignity because of the religious beliefs of the victims or their tormentors—are occurring in the twenty-first century with increasing frequency.

The 2011 Pew Forum report demonstrated that Christian communities around the world—particularly in a number of Muslim-majority countries—are cruelly victimized by religious repression. Christians are harassed, according to the report, in some 130 nations worldwide.

Muslims are close behind, suffering ill treatment in some 117 nations, many of them Muslim-majority nations. According to Grim and Finke, Muslims are harassed and persecuted in seven of every ten Muslim-majority countries (whereas they suffer harassment in just three of ten Christian-majority countries). Often the Muslim victims are from disfavored minority sects, such as the Shi'a of Saudi Arabia, or the Baha'i of Iran, who are considered to be Muslim apostates by the majority. Sometimes the victims are members of a numerical majority ruled by a tyrannical minority, such as Iraqi Shi'a under the Sunni-backed regime of Saddam Hussein or Syrian Sunnis under the Alawite regime of Bashar al-Assad.

Indeed, the religious lives of Muslims are often subject to totalitarian levels of state scrutiny and outright control. For example, in Jordan, a country that is often touted as moderate, all mosques are controlled by the government, whether they are publicly or privately funded, and all imams are civil servants paid by the state. Similarly, in Malaysia, an electoral democracy and another Muslim-majority country considered a model of moderation, only Sunni Islam is officially permitted. According to the *New York Times*, "Other forms, including Shiite Islam, are considered deviant and are not allowed to be spread." One Shiite, Mohammad

Shah, "was one of 130 Shiites detained by the religious authorities in December [2010] as they observed Ashura, the Shiite holy day commemorating the death of the Prophet Muhammad's grandson Ali, in their prayer room in an outer suburb of Kuala Lumpur."[85]

It is difficult to imagine liberal democratic norms taking root in such circumstances. A powerful obstacle to the consolidation of Muslim democracies is the persecution of Muslim reformers from both majority and minority sects. For example, reformers from the majority Sunni tradition have been charged with blasphemy—a capital crime—in Afghanistan and Pakistan for arguing that the Qur'an supports the legal equality of women with men or of non-Muslims with Muslims. This kind of religious repression not only represents a humanitarian tragedy. It also silences liberal voices, those who seek to draw upon Islam's rationalist tradition or to provide a liberal exegesis of the Qur'an. Such repression virtually ensures the dominance of extremist political theologies in public discourse.

Christian and other minorities have much to gain from the global expansion of religious freedom, but Muslims clearly do as well—both Muslim victims of persecution, and Muslim-majority nations seeking to make democracy work. Hundreds of millions of the world's Muslims will remain repressed and disempowered until their religious freedom is fully respected. Pleading the cause of religious freedom is pleading on their behalf as much as it is pleading on behalf of any persecuted minority, Christian or otherwise.

As a strategic matter, advocating the religious freedom of Muslims is advocating the success of democracy and the liberation of voices that can undermine violent Islamist extremism and terrorism.

The Effects of Religious Repression

Against this background, what can we say about what happens when powerful religious resurgence meets severe political repression? There is no iron law, no inevitability. But a general relationship is clear. Those societies where religious individuals and communities ardently seek public voice and social space and yet are systematically thwarted are precisely those societies that have tended to incubate the Islamist terrorist networks threatening global stability and American security.

Of course, religious repression does not always yield violent religious extremism and terrorism. Some groups and whole communities are subject to severe persecution over long periods of time, yet they eschew violence. Some pursue strategies of accommodation, as did numerous Orthodox churches under Communist rule throughout the former Soviet Union and Eastern Europe. Others resort to nonviolent protest.

But while religious repression is not the whole story behind the genesis of terrorist violence and extremism, it is an essential part of the story. Based on their extensive analysis of dozens of cases, sociologists Brian Grim and Roger Finke confirm a strong relationship between religion-based terrorism and a lack of religious freedom. Regimes marked by respect for religious freedom are far more resistant to violent religious extremism in the form of terrorism.

Moreover, virtually all extremist organizations in Muslim-majority countries seek to impose a radical form of Islam on their societies. The first enemy of these organizations is not America or the West but religious freedom itself. Grim and Finke found that

> the aim of the terrorist organizations within Muslim-majority countries was—in all cases analyzed—to establish either an Islamic state or domination for their particular brand of Islam. The aim of most terrorist organizations within Muslim-majority countries is not to launch attacks on the West, though this does occur, but rather to claim their country for a particular interpretation of Islam.[86]

Some terrorist groups pose a national threat, but not a global one, such as Basque separatist terrorists. Currently, those groups that pose a broader regional or global threat almost always have a prior agenda that opposes religious freedom. If a group opposes religious freedom in a Muslim-majority country, there is a good chance that it will pose a threat to the United States and global security. William Inboden, a former senior director on the National Security Council staff, and now a diplomatic historian at the University of Texas at Austin, makes this striking observation:

> Those actors with the most egregious religious freedom violations are remarkably consonant with those that pose a potential threat to the United States. This suggests that there might be more of a relationship between these two issues—religious freedom and national security—than is commonly appreciated. Stated simply, *there is not a single nation in the world that both respects religious freedom and poses a security threat to the United States.*[87]

Unsurprisingly, the nations that pose the greatest security threat to the United States tend to be those that most severely restrict religious freedom. Grim and Finke find that the most religiously restrictive Muslim-majority countries are a breeding ground for terrorism. According to Brian Grim, "much of the cross-national religious persecution categorized as religion-related terrorism has roots in religiously restrictive countries such as Saudi Arabia, Pakistan, and Yemen."[88]

There seem to be at least two reasons for this, both of which hinge on a lack of religious freedom.

The first reason concerns what might be called normative order. The regime in question officially establishes the principle that the state should prefer or impose one particular religious vision. The normative order and the legitimacy of the regime rest on a particular understanding of religion. The state and the regime are legitimate *only* to the extent that they are faithful to the established religious orthodoxy. This notion of religious legitimacy is intrinsically vulnerable and invites challenge. Any group that can plausibly claim that the government and its policies fall short of religious orthodoxy has a basis for challenging—and perhaps even overthrowing—the government. Any group whose orthodoxy is more pure, and that has enough weapons, can pose a serious and—what is important here—*legitimate* threat.

It is precisely to the extent that regimes deny religious freedom and embrace a form of religion-state integration in the first place that they invite radical challengers to initiate a violent cycle of what international security specialist Monica Duffy Toft calls "religious outbidding."[89] Such dynamics are not accidental but endemic to religiously unfree regimes.

The second reason is one of space and voice. Religiously unfree regimes offer little space and little voice for religious ideas that differ from the official, established orthodoxy. If a group wishes to exercise any kind of serious influence in such a context, it may conclude that it has no choice but to resort to violence—either with the simple and immediate goal of making its voice heard or with the strategic and long-term goal of reforming or even overthrowing the government and the entire regime.

Ten years after the 9/11 attacks, it is essential to recognize that a crucial contributor to the religious radicalism that gave rise to al Qaeda is the political repression and manipulation of Islam that is endemic in many Muslim-majority societies, especially in the Middle East. Even where some of these societies have selectively democratized, they have done so in ways that have preserved or deepened the disenfranchisement of religious citizens and religious groups, further undermining their civic independence or depriving them of any effective civic voice. Such systematic and ongoing assaults on religious freedom are a major contributor to deepening turmoil and proliferating terrorism in Muslim communities around the world.

Full Religious Freedom Supports
Democracy and Undermines Terrorism

The analysis thus far leads to important hypotheses about the relationship between religious freedom and strategic interests. When governments and powerful groups fail to honor the religious striving of individuals and communities and protect its full and free expression in a society, even if they do not directly interfere with people's private religious beliefs and practices, they weaken religious and political reformers who oppose violent extremism or authoritarian regimes or both.

Conversely, when the laws and practices of a society grant religious actors both social space and public voice, those actors are much less likely to turn to violent extremism or terrorism. As we noted, when religious actors and ideas are invited into the democratic public square, they have an opportunity to shape social norms, laws and policies, but they are also constrained by the limits imposed by liberal democracy. Just as importantly, they are forced to defend in a free marketplace of ideas—both secular and religious—their understanding of principles such as justice, freedom, equality, and the common good.

Consider how very different religious freedom policies yielded different results with respect to combating religious terrorism. Russia continues to face Islamist terrorism, particularly from Chechnya and Dagestan. Russia's religion policy since the 1990s has been to fortify the dominant status of the Orthodox Church and to limit the freedom of other religious groups. Muslims are confined to official, registered mosques, but the 3,537 of these do not come close to accommodating Russia's Muslim population of between 14 and 21 million people. Muslims are rarely given a voice in government policies.

Furthermore, Russia's response to militancy and secessionism has been a scorched-earth policy, particularly in Chechnya and Dagestan. Russia's Muslim community as a whole is routinely denounced as "Wahhabi," which has become Russian shorthand for any form of political Islam, whether militant or peaceful. As a consequence Muslims have been further alienated and victimized, and terrorist violence and secessionism continue to escalate in a vicious cycle.[90]

In Tokyo, in March 1995 members of the Aum Shinrikyo religious group conducted a terrorist attack using sarin gas in the subway system, killing a dozen people and causing hundreds of illnesses. In response, the Japanese government took immediate action to investigate Aum's activities and arrested all the individuals directly involved in criminal behavior. But they did not outlaw or ban Aum, nor did the government pass general laws targeting suspect religious groups. A move to apply the Japanese Anti-Subversive Activities Act to Aum was rejected by the Diet. One result of Japan's circumspection and continued commitment to religious freedom, according to Grim and Finke, is that "Aum has not successfully conducted further attacks, its current leader has renounced violence, and its membership has drastically decreased. The instrumental role of religious freedom in defusing the violent side of Aum seems to be clear."[91]

As the contrasting cases of Russia and Japan suggest, religious freedom can be a highly effective way to pre-empt, contain, or isolate religion's destructive manifestations as well as to encourage its constructive tendencies. Religious freedom does not assume that religion is always or inherently good. On the contrary, it recognizes that religion can assume destructive forms and that it is frequently corrupted by too close an association with political power. Religious freedom is consistent with the imposition of reasonable limits on public expressions of religion.

Religious liberty can be a means to channel religious passions and energies in constructive directions, and to check destructive religious expressions. It can help by creating a free marketplace of ideas in which all nonviolent religious alternatives and expressions are not only liberated but are also required to compete for social allegiance and political influence with other religious and non-religious alternatives.

Such an open marketplace makes it less likely that religious groups will turn to violence for lack of an alternative means of influencing society, and it ensures that democratic and liberal religious and secular voices are free to challenge undemocratic and illiberal religious voices. A policy of religious freedom tends to remove the oxygen that violent extremism needs in order to catch fire—and to spread across whole societies as well as across international borders.

Are these hypotheses applicable to Islam, especially Muslim-majority nations? Some might object that Islam is a special case, that it is Islam itself, or Islamic doctrines of a certain kind, that are the real cause of Islamist extremism and terrorism.[92] As we have noted, such doctrines reject religious freedom, and are unlikely to be altered even by a free market of religious ideas.

We reject the notion that Islam is intrinsically incapable of religious freedom or liberal democracy. We caution against a closed-minded pessimism that fails to credit the history of a rational tradition within Islam, the many emerging voices for freedom among observant Islamic nations worldwide, or the important democratic experiments ongoing in several Muslim-majority states—especially in Turkey and Indonesia, but also in Egypt, Pakistan, Iraq, and Afghanistan. [93] It is significant that some dozen Muslim states were scored in the Pew Forum report as having low levels of restriction on religion, although all but one were outside the Arab world.[94] The kind of strategic religious realism we advocate in this essay requires both prudence and a clear-eyed openness to the possibilities of political and religious progress.

Prudence also requires close attention to the fact that, as the 9/11 Report notes, violent and extremist Islamist interpretations have significant influence in many Muslim-majority states. But religious freedom can have an impact on the way those doctrines are addressed and developed.

History provides an example. In 1965 the Roman Catholic Church's Second Vatican Council promulgated its *Declaration on Religious Liberty*. That document represented the Church's demand for universal religious freedom—an immunity from coercion in religious matters for all people. It argued both that religious liberty is necessary to human flourishing and human dignity, and that it is desired by God. While continuing to demand *libertas ecclesiae*, the freedom of the Church, it now insisted that the same right be accorded all religious communities on a basis of full equality.[95]

As the Declaration itself noted, the Church had come late to an embrace of religious freedom in full for all. Its teaching was the product of doctrinal development and new historical circumstances. In the eighteenth and nineteenth centuries the Church had resisted the kind of religious liberty represented by the Enlightenment, the French Revolution, the German *Kulturkampf*, and the Italian *Risorgimento*, which were seen as anti-Catholic and leading toward religious indifferentism. But the twentieth century brought dramatic changes, including the experience of the Holocaust and the emerging consensus on religious freedom reflected in the 1948 Universal Declaration on Human Rights.

More to the point, the new historical circumstances also included the experience of religious freedom by Catholics as a minority in the United States. That experience was transmitted to the Church worldwide by Catholic intellectuals such as Jacques Maritain and the American political theologian John Courtney Murray.[96] Murray in particular laid the philosophical and theological basis for the development of doctrine that emerged in the 1965 *Declaration on Religious Liberty*.

Catholicism and Islam, of course, are very different. Their doctrines and ecclesiastical structures differ in deep and profound ways. However, the influence on Catholicism of America's system of religious freedom suggests that history can influence doctrinal development, even amid resistance, provided that the theological seed is present in the tradition. In Catholicism, the seed was there in the New Testament ("Render unto Caesar"), the fifth-century Gelasian doctrine of two authorities (ruler and priest), the writings on conscience of medieval canonists and scholastics, and the early modern defense of the human rights of native Americans by Catholic thinkers such as Bartolomé de las Casas.[97]

The seed also appears to be present in Islam. It is there in the traditions of rationalism that, according to Mustafa Akyol, developed in early Islamic history and have never been eradicated. It is there in the modern writings of scholars such as Abdullah and Hassan Saeed, who locate an obligation to protect religious freedom for all squarely in the sacred scriptures of Islam—the Qur'an.[98]

In the final analysis, there is no certainty about whether nations influenced by Islamic thought will adopt religious freedom and liberal democracy. But the possibility exists, and it should be encouraged by all nations that desire success for Muslim democracies and a world free of Islamist terror.

Try a thought experiment. Imagine that Osama bin Laden and the fifteen Saudi hijackers of 9/11 were born and raised in a Saudi Arabia that protected religious liberty. Instead of being steeped exclusively in the toxic teachings of Wahhabism and Sayyid Qutb, they would have been exposed to religious arguments for justice, freedom, equality, and the common good—arguments posed by Shiites, non-Wahhabi Sunni Muslims, Christians, Jews, Hindus, atheists, and secularists. Whatever their ideas about public matters, bin Laden and the others would have had to develop and defend those ideas in discourse with alternative views.

Had Saudi Arabia been a land of religious freedom, would 9/11 have happened?

Conclusion

Why is it in America's interest, and in the interest of all freedom-loving nations, that religious freedom spread? Because we know from hard experience that we cannot long prosper in a world that is deficient in this and other fundamental human rights. We learned that lesson from two terrible world wars. We learned that lesson during a long Cold War.

Every government has an interest in securing the religious freedom of its people as a means of safeguarding its stability and defusing extremism and terrorism.

No nation can enjoy long-term security unless the Muslim-majority world enjoys long-term liberty. This is true because societies subject to prolonged and systematic violations of religious freedom are either deeply and chronically unstable, breeding grounds of extremism and terrorism, or both.

Strategy means choosing, from among all the good and right things we could choose, those that are best, not only because they are good and right but because they advance our most compelling interests. A policy of promoting international religious freedom cannot be sustained if it is not sound strategy and if it is not in the interest of the country promoting it.

As it happens, it is both.

CHAPTER SEVEN

The Strategic Dimension:
Policy Implications

The active promotion of religious freedom is a wise course for all governments seeking to advance global peace, security, and self-government grounded in ordered liberty. Religious liberty in the twenty-first century is embattled in ways that threaten a wide circle of goods and interests, including democracy, economic growth, social stability, and the fight against religion-based violence, extremism, and terrorism.

As we have seen, religious liberty is a constituent element of the interlocking web of fundamental rights that make democracy liberal, stable, and lasting. In the last decades of the twentieth century, democracy spread rapidly in many parts of the world. But many of the new polities were "electoral democracies," that is, they were capable of conducting free and fair elections, but they lacked key elements of the interlocking web—especially religious liberty.[99] Some made advances in the other fundamental rights (for example, freedom of secular speech or of secular association), but lagged badly in protecting the right of religious freedom.

The challenges to religious freedom outside the West might be categorized as threats from governments and societies that are either theocratic or "seculocratic," and from a host of radical movements. Here the humanitarian dimensions of the problem are catastrophic, with tens of millions of people subject to violent persecution. But the security implications are equally grim: the absence of religious freedom decreases the chances that struggling democracies can be successful, or that religion-based terrorism can be defeated.

- **Theocracy.** These are societies in which the state works closely with a single religion to impose a *de jure* or *de facto* social and political monopoly. In these societies, according to Grim and Finke, "religious freedom faces severe restrictions from both the government and society." Familiar examples include Iran, Sudan, and Saudi Arabia. Another is Burma, whose authoritarian military junta actively promotes—but also manipulates—Theravada Buddhism. In most theocratic states, such as Iran, it is not only minority communities such as Baha'is and Christians who suffer restriction and persecution.

In the Islamic Republic of Iran, reformist Shiites whose brand of the faith differs from that of the theocratic regime are banned from publishing, beaten by government supporters, and imprisoned. The 14 countries with effective religious monopolies are home to some 760 million people, or well over 10 percent of the world's population, according to Grim and Finke.[100]

- **Seculocracy.** Even more of the world's people live in countries that could be classified as *seculocratic*. These are societies whose government has an identity and legitimacy independent of religion, rooted in a secular political program or a traditional dynastic monarchy. These regimes give official support to no religion but subject all to some form of systematic control. Highly repressive seculocracies include Communist regimes such as China, North Korea, and Vietnam. Syria and Turkey are also seculocracies that impose strong limits on the religious freedom of all groups. According to Grim and Finke, some 17 countries fall into this general category, representing about a billion and a half people. A few, such as Turkey, are electoral democracies.

- **Radical Movements.** At the same time, many threats to religious freedom do not come from governments, but from radical movements that operate essentially independently of states. Radical Islamist movements and ideologies, such as the Taliban in Afghanistan, Sipah-e-Sabha in Pakistan, and al Qaeda and its affiliates operating in numerous countries, are the most prevalent and powerful of these non-state radical movements in the world today. Their violent attacks frequently target and terrorize religious groups and houses of worship, robbing them of their freedom to practice their faith and even to exist as viable communities. Christians, Shiites, Jews, Hindus, Ahmadis, and Baha'is are some of the groups that have been the focus of vicious attacks by radical Islamist groups, resulting in some cases in the religious cleansing of neighborhoods, districts, and—gradually—even entire countries and regions. But Islamist groups are not the only villains. For example, radical Hindu movements regularly terrorize religious minorities in India, most recently in Orissa state, where in 2008 Hindu-nationalist assaults killed dozens of people and left some 50,000 Christians homeless.

The global erosion of religious freedom creates a truly international crisis that requires a far more effective international response. The response must be as wide-ranging and global as the crisis itself.

Part of the challenge is to convince the skeptics, and others who downplay or oppose religious freedom, that it is in their interest to protect this human right, even if doing so will empower those with whom they disagree. These skeptics exist all over the world, in every society, and in every form of government. They are certainly there in theocracies, seculocracies, and extremist movements, but they are also there in Western democracies.

Wherever the skeptics reside, however, and whatever the reason for their skepticism, they must square their views with the foundational principle of justice and democracy: equality under the law. This means that in disputes over political matters, individuals and groups cannot be required to leave their religious beliefs and arguments at the door before entering the public square.

A number of conclusions follow from the foregoing analysis. One is that all nations must reexamine, or (as the case may be) engage in earnest for the first time, the question of where religious freedom fits into their concepts of justice and national interest. When they conclude that it fits squarely into both—as the United States and Canada have done, and others seem poised to do—those nations must incorporate the advancement of religious freedom into their foreign policies. We offer below some specific recommendations on how this might be done.

But the global shifts we endorse in this chapter cannot be accomplished by governments alone. Often culture drives politics, which means that societies must come to understand the value of religious freedom. The reasons they should do so are addressed elsewhere in this book, but the recommendations that follow take those reasons into account. At the most general level, we recommend that governments do all they can to empower indigenous actors—both religious and secular—who value religious liberty for all people.

This means that the foreign policy structures of particular nations such as the United States must be strengthened in their capacity to work effectively with other countries and international institutions to coordinate a more robust response to global violations of religious freedom. It also means that the world's religious communities must work together in a way that is more coordinated and institutionalized to identify the global threats to religious freedom and forge common responses where possible. Religious communities can and must work more effectively to promote cooperation on religious freedom both within particular countries and internationally.

This also means that existing international agencies must be strengthened in their capacity to address religious freedom.

Recommendations:

- Give the religious freedom function an appropriately robust status within the foreign policy community.

    In the United States the 1998 International Religious Freedom Act (IRFA) established in the Department of State an ambassador-at-large for international religious freedom with the mission of advancing religious freedom using the tools of U.S. foreign policy.

    No American administration has given the IRF ambassador-at-large the authority, status, or resources necessary to accomplish this mission. The ambassador should be situated in the office of the Secretary of State, and should report to the Secretary. This was the status intended by the IRFA and is the status historically granted most other U.S. ambassadors-at-large. Under the Obama administration, for example, the ambassadors-at-large for Global Women's Issues, War Crimes, and Counter-Terrorism reported directly to the Secretary of State. Elevating the status of the IRF ambassador will communicate to foreign officials and American officials alike that the United States gives a high priority to the advancement of international religious freedom. At present, neither group of officials believes this to be the case.

As other nations decide whether and how to establish a foreign policy of advancing international religious freedom, they should ensure that the official who heads that policy is given sufficient status to be seen as a senior official within the domestic diplomatic establishment, and by foreign governments.

- Give religious freedom policymakers sufficient resources.

The United States Congress has not provided independent appropriations for the ambassador-at-large for international religious freedom or for the ambassador's office. This has severely restricted the ability of the ambassador to develop strategies that can be successful. Nations must provide appropriate funding, not only for staff and operations, but also for programs that can achieve the objectives identified in this chapter.

One model for such programs is the National Endowment for Democracy. That organization has for decades been funded by Congress to implant the institutions and habits of democracy. Until recently, few of those funds have been targeted at advancing religious freedom, and current expenditures tend to be made on an *ad hoc* basis with no strategic direction. The foreign policy official responsible for advancing international religious freedom (in the U.S. case, the ambassador-at-large) should have authority over this kind of funding in order to increase the opportunities for success.

- Even more importantly, governments should adopt a broad approach to advancing international religious freedom. In the United States, for example, the ambassador should develop international religious freedom strategies in parallel with a broader religious engagement policy, including diplomatic efforts to undermine religion-based terrorism and to promote stable democracy and economic development. The successful development and implementation of new religious freedom strategies will require new training and incentives for diplomats, integration of religious freedom into U.S. public diplomacy, and the consistent prioritization of religious freedom within annual State Department and embassy program planning.
- During national election cycles, all candidates (especially presidential candidates) should be pressed about their position on international religious freedom policy, and urged to announce their intention to implement the recommendations mentioned above and below.
- Specifically, we recommend that the United States government:

  o Institute a religion/religious freedom subspecialty under the political, economic, and public diplomacy career tracks for Foreign Service Officers.
  o Mandate, in the president's letter of instruction to U.S. ambassadors, the allocation of embassy resources to engage religious actors, ideas, and communities, and to advance religious freedom broadly understood.

o Require every U.S. mission abroad, and every regional bureau at the Department of State, to develop a religious freedom strategy as part of its annual program planning.
o Integrate religious freedom into all U.S. democracy planning and programs, such as those at the U.S. Agency for International Development and the National Endowment for Democracy.
o Provide a representative from the State Department IRF office to all counterterrorism agencies. The IRF ambassador-at-large should serve as a special assistant to the president on religion and national security issues. Assign a senior advisor on counterterrorism to the IRF ambassador-at-large.
o Integrate the office of the IRF ambassador-at-large into all strategic and operational decisions regarding democracy promotion and programming.
o Encourage the U.S. Commission on International Religious Freedom to continue and expand its efforts to study the effects of religious freedom on religious extremism.
o Support, via foreign aid and democracy funding, religious and secular non-governmental organizations (NGOs) around the world that seek to advance religious freedom as part of democratic development.
o Encourage existing public and private diplomatic institutions to increase interfaith dialogues and exchanges.
o Expand programming on religious freedom in public diplomacy, and in radio, television, and other media under the Broadcasting Board of Governors.
o Seek the counsel of religious actors and groups who have deep experience in target cultures, as well as American-based clerics and scholars, in order to increase American understanding of extremist and terrorist groups and how to defeat them.
o Increase the administration's commitment to international human rights monitoring institutions, including those that monitor and report on human rights and religious freedom in the United States.
o Encourage the U.S. Commission on International Religious Freedom to monitor the administration's progress toward integrating IRF policy into the mainstream of diplomacy.

• The U.S. Congress should provide regular oversight over the implementation of IRFA to ensure that the mandate of the law is followed. Congressional committees on foreign affairs should create subcommittees on international religious freedom.
• The office of the United Nations Special Rapporteur on Freedom of Religion or Belief should receive significantly greater funding and staffing and a wider mandate to conduct research on global challenges to religious freedom, and to make recommendations to the United Nations.

- U.S. leadership on religious freedom in multilateral institutions should be invigorated. The United States should place a senior International Religious Freedom official in the U.S. mission to the UN.
- Advocacy for religious freedom should transcend any one religious group. We propose that the world's major religious communities work together, whether in a coalition or in a new international, non-governmental organization, to promote religious freedom on an ecumenical basis. This would send the message that religious freedom is not the special pleading of any one group but is the common, non-negotiable demand of human dignity, of religious integrity, and of the wholeness and health of the civic community. Such a coalition or organization would be an investigative body independent of any and all governments and political movements, yet one that actively seeks to spotlight and influence the actions and policies of governments and political movements.

Conclusion

Despite the predictions of secularization theory, religious faith stirs the hearts and forms the consciences of great proportions of the global population. In fact, some of the most influential proponents of secularization theory concede that the world as a whole has more people with traditional religious views than ever before, and, what is more, "they constitute a growing proportion of the world's population."[101]

Even where people are not religious in a conventional sense, they frequently have deeply held convictions about ultimate reality. Perhaps they believe that all of life is somehow sacred. Perhaps they are deeply convinced that every person has a god-like freedom and dignity. Perhaps they believe that a benevolent, pervasive force or spirit suffuses the universe. In any case, such convictions are deeply held. And they are religious.

Amid basic disagreements of theology, therefore, the world's religious believers have something significant in common: they seek to achieve some kind of harmony with the deepest foundations of reality. They seek access to an ultimate, other-than-human order. And many believe they have been given enough of an understanding of this order to make a difference in their lives and in the societies in which they live.

The argument of this essay is that religious freedom demands the world's respect and deserves its protection. What this means is clear.

It means that no earthly power has the right to stand in the way of a man's pursuit of religious truth. No authority on earth has the right to hinder or manipulate a woman as she seeks to explore, embrace, and express the truth in accordance with the promptings of her conscience.

Every person has the right to engage all the dimensions of personhood—physical and spiritual, communal and individual, public and private—in the quest to be faithful to the divine. Every person has the right to adhere inwardly to those religious convictions commended by conscience, as well as the right to express and manifest these convictions, both alone and together with others.

This is religious freedom.

To return to the two questions with which we began this essay:

- What reasons do we have, if any, for thinking that all people everywhere enjoy a right to religious freedom so understood? *In other words, is religious freedom really universal?*
- Even if there is such a right, what reasons do we have, if any, for caring very much about whether the religious freedom of people is respected or not? *In other words, is religious freedom really urgent?*

This essay introduced distinct streams of research and reflection to give a clear and compelling answer to both questions: yes, religious freedom is both a universal imperative and an urgent global issue.

From psychology and other social sciences we know that religious impulses and beliefs appear early, easily, and frequently in human beings. They appear in the macro-development of human civilization, as the 12,000-year-old temple discovered at Göbekli Tepe in Turkey suggests. And they appear in the micro-development of human individuals, as the cumulative insights of the cognitive science of religion suggest.

Thinkers of the French Enlightenment such as Voltaire argued that religion was an artifice foisted on gullible people by a wicked clerical establishment—an artifice so irrational that it would quickly disappear as the light of science spread and the power of priests waned. But anthropological research suggests that more or less the opposite is true: the structures of human thought naturally and easily invite a religious orientation to the world. And the stubbornness of religious belief, even in the face of concerted political programs of secularization, and the comparative rarity of thoroughly secular societies, suggest that such a religious orientation is overcome only with some difficulty, under exceptional historical and cultural circumstances. Religion, in short, is a pervasive and natural feature of human experience.

From sociology, economics, political science, and history, we know that societies characterized by strong forms of religious freedom are typically characterized by the enjoyment of other freedoms, by significant protections of legal equality for women and minorities, by the rule of law, by political stability, and by improvements in economic prosperity and other measures of social development. Religious freedom, whether it is cause or effect of these other goods, seems inseparable from them. Societies that give the natural and pervasive religious tendencies of human beings ample breathing room are far more prosperous and free and far less divisive and violent.

Philosophical reflection on principles of morality enables us to discern the reasons for the protection of religious freedom in basic notions of human flourishing. We can see that religious freedom is not just the culturally relative preference of certain societies with certain historical backgrounds, but a cross-cultural principle of justice itself. Human persons have an intrinsic interest in forming their characters and lives into integrated wholes that fully reflect the implications of the truth about ultimate reality. Anything less than full religious freedom fails to respect the dignity of persons as free truth-seekers, acting in accord with their own judgments of conscience. And anything less than full religious freedom fails to respect the proper integrity and authenticity of human persons.

Religious reflection itself leads to similar conclusions. Not only the major Abrahamic traditions of Judaism, Christianity, and Islam, but the very nature of religion demands robust respect for the principles of religious freedom. Taken together, the various religious arguments for religious freedom converge in a remarkable way around a core proposition—namely, that faith is not faith unless it is free. The core religious argument for religious freedom is that freedom is religion's essential precondition. Coercion in matters of faith does not merely violate religion; it nullifies religion. Freedom for faith does not merely honor religion. It makes religion possible.

But how is religious freedom to be protected? This is in part an empirical question, intertwined with questions of legal principle and practical statesmanship. Much can be gained here from reflection on historical experience: what is the place and status of religious freedom in the constitutions, laws, and legal traditions of the United States, of other countries, and of the international community? Does respect for religious freedom enjoy a place in the laws of only a few countries or many countries? What place has religious freedom taken in international law?

Legal principles are not, in the final analysis, self-executing. It is easy to put religious freedom "down on paper," but while this is important, what James Madison called "parchment barriers" to tyranny are not sufficient. Statesmanship, in the domestic life of nations and in their global relations with one another, demands that religious freedom be treated as a living thing to be nurtured, fed, and spread if it is to survive and flourish.

In the making and administration of law, in the adjudication of legal principles, and in the fields of diplomacy, rhetorical leadership, and the practical application of all the tools of international statecraft, the protection and fostering of religious freedom are matters of the first importance for responsible public officials.

Much of the "strategic" discussion in the foregoing pages has focused on the threats to religious freedom that rear their heads in the non-Western world, particularly in the "Muslim arc" that extends from the western Mediterranean to the island nations of the Indian and Pacific oceans. But Western political leaders have no cause to preen about the superiority of their own societies in this respect, for the West has its own homegrown problems with deeply troubling implications.

A Western Coda

In the West, religious freedom faces growing threats from judges, politicians, and whole populations that are seeking to curb religious expression and relegate religious actors and ideas to the margins of public life.

Perhaps these seemingly distant examples risk giving readers from established Western democracies the impression that "it can't happen here." Surely, unlike in Iran or in China, religious freedom in countries such as the United States, Canada, Britain, France, and Germany is safe and secure? Surely, these free societies are immune to serious threats to religious liberty?

Think again.

- In Britain, Eunice and Owen Johns applied to the Derby City Council in 2007 to foster a child. The Council blocked their application because the Johnses—who are Christians—could not in conscience agree to teach a young child that homosexual acts are morally acceptable. In November 2010 both parties asked the High Court of England and Wales to rule on whether the Johnses were able to foster children, or whether they could be excluded from doing so under equality law because of their religious beliefs. In a landmark judgment on February 28, 2011, the High Court ruled that laws protecting people from discrimination because of their sexual orientation "should take precedence" over the right to be free from religious discrimination. If children are placed with foster parents who object to homosexuality, the Court determined that "there may well be a conflict with the local authority's duty to 'safeguard and promote the welfare' of . . . children."[102]
- On April 30, 2007, the Sexual Orientation Regulations came into force in the United Kingdom, requiring adoption agencies in receipt of public funds to open their services to same-sex couples. Though pressed to make an exception for religious adoption agencies, and though three Catholic Cabinet ministers ultimately resigned over the issue, the Government refused to grant any exemptions. In an ultimatum he called a "compromise," Prime Minister Tony Blair gave religious adoption agencies two years to adapt or close. A high court judge ordered Britain's Charity Commission to reconsider its decision. But the Commission concluded in August 2010 that respect for religious views does not justify discrimination against gays because of the public nature of adoption services.
- In a November 2009 Swiss referendum, a constitutional amendment banning the construction of new minarets was approved by 57.5 percent of participating voters. Only four of the 26 Swiss cantons, mostly in the French-speaking part of Switzerland, opposed the initiative. Many Swiss Muslims are affected by the ban. One group especially affected is the Ahmadiyya, who face vicious persecution in many Muslim-majority countries and therefore seek refuge and asylum in Western societies such as Switzerland. One Ahmadiyya mosque has the first minaret erected in Switzerland. The ban now prevents Ahmadi believers from constructing any more mosques in accordance with their religious convictions and practices.
- In the United States, on March 10, 2006, Catholic Charities of Boston was given the choice of ceasing its adoption services—which it had operated for over a century as part of its religious mission—or abandoning a central

teaching of Roman Catholicism. Unable to choose the latter course, it was forced to stop handling adoptions after a Massachusetts law barring discrimination based on sexual orientation was applied through a licensing procedure. State legislators refused to provide any accommodation for the charity to honor its religious beliefs. In the legislature's view, the issue was not that Catholic Charities received government funds but that it was providing a service inherently subject to state regulation.

These threats and the many more that have been documented in recent reports and studies demonstrate that "[r]eligious freedom may be our 'first freedom,' but it is also our most embattled."[103]

For all those men and women whose stories began this essay, and for the sake of all mankind, the nations of the world must renew their commitment to the protection of religious freedom. It is the call of conscience on us all.

Let us give that persistent Quaker woman, Mary Dyer, hanged on Boston Commons in 1660, the last word:

"My life not availeth me in comparison to the liberty of the truth."

The Witherspoon Institute's Task Force on International Religious Freedom

We gratefully acknowledge
the generous support of
The William E. Simon Foundation
for the work of
The William E. and Carol G. Simon
Center on Religion and the Constitution
and the
Task Force on International Religious Freedom

Thomas F. Farr, Chairman, is Visiting Associate Professor of Religion and International Affairs in the School of Foreign Service at Georgetown University, where he is also Director of the Religious Freedom Project at the Berkley Center for Religion, Peace, and World Affairs. A former American diplomat, Farr was the first director of the State Department's Office of International Religious Freedom.

Timothy Samuel Shah, principal author of this monograph, is Associate Director of the Religious Freedom Project at the Berkley Center, and Visiting Assistant Professor in the Government Department, at Georgetown University.

Matthew J. Franck, editor-in-chief of this monograph, is Director of the William E. and Carol G. Simon Center on Religion and the Constitution at the Witherspoon Institute, and Professor Emeritus of Political Science at Radford University.

Gerard V. Bradley is Professor of Law at the University of Notre Dame, and a Senior Fellow of the Witherspoon Institute, where he serves on the Board of Overseers of the Simon Center.

Jennifer S. Bryson is Director of the Islam and Civil Society Project at the Witherspoon Institute, and a former Department of Defense official.

William Inboden is Assistant Professor in the Lyndon B. Johnson School of Public Affairs at the University of Texas at Austin, and a former National Security Council staff member.

Jennifer Marshall is Director of Domestic Policy Studies and of the Richard and Helen DeVos Center for Religion and Civil Society at the Heritage Foundation.

Margarita Mooney is Assistant Professor of Sociology at the University of North Carolina at Chapel Hill and a Fellow of the Witherspoon Institute.

Joseph Wood is a former advisor on foreign policy in the administration of President George W. Bush, and a former fellow of the German Marshall Fund.

Other Contributors:

David Novak holds the J. Richard and Dorothy Shiff Chair of Jewish Studies as Professor of Religion and Philosophy at the University of Toronto.

Nicholas Wolterstorff is Noah Porter Professor of Philosophical Theology Emeritus at Yale University.

Abdullah Saeed is Sultan of Oman Professor of Arab and Islamic Studies, and Director of the National Center for Excellence for Islamic Studies at the University of Melbourne.

Notes

1. Kevin Seamus Hasson, *The Right to Be Wrong: Ending the Culture War Over Religion in America* (New York: Encounter, 2005), 40.

2. http://www.nytimes.com/2008/01/24/world/middleeast/24 afghan.html; last accessed on November 18, 2011.

3. http://www.alliancedefensefund.org/Home/ADFContent?cid=5050; last accessed on November 18, 2011.

4. United States Department of State, Bureau of Democracy, Human Rights, and Labor, *International Religious Freedom Report 2010*, November 17, 2010, "Eritrea." Available at http://www.state.gov/g/drl/rls/irf/2010/148686.htm; last accessed on November 5, 2011.

5. http://bikyamasr.com/47199/egypt-rights-committee-says-unknown-shooters-killed-coptic-christians/; last accessed on November 18, 2011.

6. Eight countries abstained.

7. Pew Forum on Religion & Public Life, "Global Restrictions on Religion," December 17, 2009, 1. Available at http://pewforum.org/Government/Global-Restrictions-on-Religion.aspx; last accessed on November 5, 2011.

8. Quintan Wiktorowicz, *The Management of Islamic Activism: Salafis, the Muslim Brotherhood, and State Power in Jordan* (Albany: State University of New York Press, 2001), 53.

9. Monica Duffy Toft, Daniel Philpott, and Timothy Samuel Shah, *God's Century: Resurgent Religion and Global Politics* (New York: W. W. Norton, 2011), 21, paraphrasing William P. Alston, "Religion," *Encyclopedia of Philosophy*, vol. 7 (New York: Macmillan, 1972), 140–45.

10. Christian Smith, *Moral, Believing Animals: Human Personhood and Culture* (New York: Oxford University Press, 2003), 98.

11. Joseph Boyle, "The Place of Religion in the Practical Reasoning of Individuals and Groups," *American Journal of Jurisprudence* 43 (1998): 3.

12. Martin Riesebrodt, *The Promise of Salvation: A Theory of Religion*, tr. Steven Rendall (Chicago: University of Chicago Press, 2010), 76, 83.

13. Justin L. Barrett, "The Naturalness and Freedom of Religion" (paper prepared for Witherspoon Institute Consultation on International Religious Freedom, May 6, 2011), 1.

14. Charles Mann, "The Birth of Religion," *National Geographic* (June 2011): 39.

15. Barrett, "The Naturalness and Freedom of Religion," 1, 2.

16. Justin L. Barrett, *Why Would Anyone Believe in God?* (Lanham, MD: AltaMira Press, 2004).

17. Jesse Bering, *The Belief Instinct: The Psychology of Souls, Destiny, and the Meaning of Life* (New York: W. W. Norton, 2011), 8, 195–96, 49.

18. Boyle, "The Place of Religion in the Practical Reasoning of Individuals and Groups," 22.

19. *Planned Parenthood of Southeastern Pa.* v. *Casey*, 505 U.S. 833 (1992), at 851 (joint opinion of O'Connor, Kennedy, and Souter, JJ.)

20. Joseph Raz, *Ethics in the Public Domain: Essays in the Morality of Law and Politics* (Oxford: Clarendon Press, 1996), 259; Nicholas Wolterstorff, *Justice: Rights and Wrongs* (Princeton: Princeton University Press, 2008), 261–63.

21. Michael Gerson, "In Search of China's Soul," *The Washington Post*, May 13, 2011, A17.

22. Brian Spegele, "China's Banned Churches Defy Regime," the *Wall Street Journal*, July 28, 2011, A1.

23. Brian J. Grim, "Is Promoting Religious Freedom Dangerous? An Essay for the Witherspoon International Religious Freedom Meeting," May 6, 2011, 15.

24. Brian J. Grim, "Is Promoting Religious Freedom Dangerous?" 17. The findings of the Hudson Institute study are presented in Brian J. Grim, "God's Economy: Religious Freedom and Socioeconomic Well-Being," in Paul Marshall, ed., *Religious Freedom in the World* (Lanham, MD: Rowman & Littlefield, 2008), 42–47.

25. Brian J. Grim, "Religious Freedom: Good For What Ails Us?" *Review of Faith & International Affairs* 6.2 (Summer 2008): 3–7.

26. Brian J. Grim and Roger Finke, *The Price of Freedom Denied: Religious Persecution and Conflict in the 21st Century* (New York: Cambridge University Press, 2011), 212. Emphasis in the original.

27. Toft, Philpott, and Shah, *God's Century*, 161–62.

28. Mohammed M. Hafez, *Why Muslims Rebel: Repression and Resistance in the Islamic World* (Boulder, CO: Lynne Rienner Publishers, 2003), 202.

29. Fabio Oliva, "Between Contribution and Disengagement: Post-conflict Elections and the OSCE Role in the Normalization of Armed Groups and Militarized Political Parties in Bosnia and Herzegovina, Tajikistan, and Kosovo," *Helsinki Monitor: Security and Human Rights* 18.3 (2007), 206. The discussion of Tajikistan here closely follows Toft, Philpott, and Shah, *God's Century*, 166–68.

30. Anthony Gill, "Response to Brian Gill's 'Is Religion Dangerous?'" (paper prepared for Witherspoon International Religious Freedom Consultation, May 6, 2011), 7.

31. President Barack Obama, Press Conference with President Obama and President Hu of the People's Republic of China, January 19, 2011. Transcript available at http://www.whitehouse.gov/the-press-office/2011/01/19/press-conference-president-obama-and-president-hu-peoples-republic-china; last accessed on November 5, 2011.

32. John Henry Newman, "A Letter Addressed to the Duke of Norfolk on Occasion of Mr. Gladstone's Recent Expostulation," *Certain Difficulties Felt by Anglicans in Catholic Teaching*, Vol. 2, Chap. V (Conscience), 1875. Available at http://www.newmanreader.org/works/anglicans/volume2/gladstone/section 5.html; last accessed on November 5, 2011.

33. John Milton, "Areopagitica," in Douglas Bush, ed., *The Portable Milton* (New York: Viking, 1949), 180.

34. Benjamin Franklin, letter to Richard Price, October 9, 1780, in Franklin, *Writings*, ed. J. A. Leo Lemay (New York: Library of America, 1987), 1031.

35. Christopher Tollefsen, "Conscience, Religion and the State," *American Journal of Jurisprudence* 54 (2009): 96.

36. John M. Finnis, *Natural Law and Natural Rights*, 2nd ed. (New York: Oxford University Press, 2011), 88.

37. Richard John Neuhaus, "A New Order of Religious Freedom," *First Things* (February 1992): 14–15. Available at http://www.firstthings.com/article/2008/01/001-a-new-order-of-religious-freedom-34; last accessed on November 5, 2011.

38. James Madison, "Memorial and Remonstrance Against Religious Assessments" (1785), in *Writings*, ed. Jack N. Rakove (New York: Library of America, 1999), 30 (emphasis added).

39. Tollefsen, "Conscience, Religion and the State," 97–98.

40. Tertullian, *Apology* 24.6–10, in Tertullian and Marcus Minucius Felix, *Apology; De spectaculis*, translated by T. R. Glover and Gerald H. Rendall (Cambridge, MA: Harvard University Press,

1931), 132–33. We are grateful to Robert Louis Wilken for the translation and for making us aware of the text.

41. Elisha Williams, "The Essential Rights and Liberties of Protestants" (1744), in Ellis Sandoz, ed., *Political Sermons of the American Founding Era, 1730–1805*, 2nd ed. (Indianapolis: Liberty Fund, 1998), 65–66.

42. Lactantius, *Divine Institutes*, Book V, Chapter 20. The translations are those of Robert Louis Wilken.

43. Tertullian, *Ad Scapulam* 2.1–2. The translation is by Robert Louis Wilken.

44. In *The Mighty and the Almighty* (New York: Cambridge University Press, forthcoming).

45. See, in particular, discussion in Abdullah Saeed and Hassan Saeed, *Freedom of Religion, Apostasy, and Islam* (Aldershot, UK: Ashgate, 2004), 21–30.

46. See *ibid.*, 93–98 for further discussion.

47. Kamali, *Freedom of Expression in Islam*, 86. Cf. Fathi `Uthman, *Huquq al Insan Bayn al-Shari'ah al-Islamiyyahwa al-Fikr al-Qanuni al-Gharbi* (Beirut: Dar al-Shurug,1982), 91.

48. Saeed and Saeed, *Freedom of Religion*, 69.

49. *Ibid.*, 72.

50. *Ibid.*, 70–71.

51. *Ibid.*, 72.

52. *Ibid.*, 73.

53. Kamali, *Freedom of Expression in Islam*, 100.

54. Saeed and Saeed, *Freedom of Religion*, 56.

55. Kamali, *Freedom of Expression in Islam*, 92.

56. *Ibid.*, 94, citing Hadith 229. Muhammad b. Isma`il Al-Bukhari, *Jawahir Sahib al-Bukhari* ed. `Izz al-Din Sirwan (Beirut: Dar al-Ihya, 1987), 150.

57. Kamali, *Freedom of Expression in Islam*, 92.

58. Saeed and Saeed, *Freedom of Religion*, 60.

59. John M. Finnis, "Darwin, Dewey, Religion, and the Public Domain," in Finnis, *Religion and Public Reasons*, vol. 5 of *Collected Essays* (New York: Oxford University Press, 2011), 17.

60. Christopher L. Eisgruber and Lawrence G. Sager, "The Vulnerability of Conscience: The Constitutional Basis for Protecting Religious Conduct," *University of Chicago Law Review* 61 (1994): 1248. Eisgruber and Sager expanded their argument in *Religious Freedom and the Constitution* (Cambridge, MA: Harvard University Press, 2007).

61. Brian Leiter, "Why Tolerate Religion?" *Constitutional Commentary* 25 (2008): 2, 26 (emphasis in original).

62. Michael W. McConnell, "The Problem of Singling Out Religion," *DePaul Law Review* 50 (2000): 42.

63. George Washington, Letter to the Hebrew Congregation of Newport, Rhode Island, August 1790. Available at http://www.teaching americanhistory.org/library/index.asp?document=21; last accessed November 18, 2011.

64. *Federalist* No. 51, in Madison, *Writings*, 297.

65. Gerard V. Bradley, *Religious Liberty in the American Republic* (Washington, DC: Heritage Foundation, 2008), 3.

66. Mary Ann Glendon, *The Forum and the Tower: How Scholars and Politicians Have Imagined the World, from Plato to Eleanor Roosevelt* (New York: Oxford University Press, 2011), 205, 206.

67. Grim and Finke, *Price of Freedom Denied*, 27.

68. There are notable exceptions, of course. For example, in Saudi Arabia the constitution is the Qur'an as interpreted by the radical Wahhabi sect. In Pakistan and elsewhere in the Middle East, anti-blasphemy and anti-apostasy laws are, on their face, opposed to religious freedom. See Paul Marshall and Nina Shea, *Silenced: How Blasphemy and Apostasy Codes Are Choking Freedom Worldwide* (New York: Oxford, 2011).

69. President Franklin Roosevelt, "Four Freedoms Speech," Annual Message to Congress on the State of the Union, January 6, 1941. Available at http://www.fdrlibrary.marist.edu/pdfs/fftext.pdf; last accessed on November 5, 2011.

70. Universal Declaration of Human Rights, Article 18. Available at http://www.un.org/en/documents/udhr/. Last accessed on November 5, 2011. On the role of Eleanor Roosevelt and Charles Malik in the framing of the Universal Declaration, see Mary Ann Glendon, *A World Made New: Eleanor Roosevelt and the Universal Declaration of Human Rights* (New York: Random House, 2001).

71. Allen D. Hertzke, *Freeing God's Children: The Unlikely Alliance for Global Human Rights* (Lanham, MD: Rowman & Littlefield, 2004); Thomas F. Farr, *World of Faith and Freedom: Why International Religious Liberty Is Vital to American National Security* (New York: Oxford University Press, 2008), chaps. 4–7.

72. National Security Strategy of the United States 2006, Chapter II: "Champion Aspirations for Human Dignity" (emphasis added). Available at http://georgewbush-whitehouse.archives.gov/nsc/nss/2006/; last accessed on November 5, 2011.

73. "Harper promotes religious freedom office," April 23, 2011, CBC News (available at http://www.cbc.ca/news/politics/canadavotes2011/story/2011/04/23/cv-election-harper-saturday.html; last accessed on November 5, 2011); "Address by Minister Baird at Office of Religious Freedom Stakeholder Consultations," October 3, 2011 (available at http://www.international.gc.ca/media/aff/speeches-discours/2011/2011-034.aspxlang=eng&view=d; last accessed on November 5, 2011); "Merkel vows to fight for religious freedom," January 8, 2011, Associated Press (available at http://www.jpost.com/Headlines/Article.aspx?id=202672; last accessed on November 18, 2011).

74. National Commission on Terrorist Attacks Upon the United States, *The 9/11 Commission Report: Final Report of the National Commission on Terrorist Attacks Upon the United States* (New York: W. W. Norton, 2004), 362.

75. See Mustafa Akyol, *Islam Without Extremes: A Muslim Case for Liberty* (New York: W. W. Norton, 2011); Saeed and Saeed, *Freedom of Religion*.

76. For discussion of some of these cases, and a typology of religious restrictions, see Grim and Finke, *Price of Freedom Denied*, 82–86, 121–40.

77. Toft, Philpott, and Shah, *God's Century*, 133–35.

78. Anthony Gill, *Rendering Unto Caesar: The Catholic Church and the State in Latin America* (Chicago: University of Chicago Press, 1998); Grim and Finke, *Price of Freedom Denied*, 171–74; Toft, Philpott, and Shah, *God's Century*, 82–120.

79. The following section is adapted from Timothy Samuel Shah and Monica Toft, "God is Winning: Religion in Global Politics," in Paul A. Marshall, Lela Gilbert, and Roberta Green, eds., *Blind Spot: When Journalists Don't Get Religion* (New York: Oxford University Press, 2009), pp. 11-30. See also Farr, *World of Faith and Freedom*, 24–28.

80. Arnold Toynbee, "Preface," in John Cogley, *Religion in a Secular Age: The Search for Final Meaning* (New York: Praeger, 1968), xix (emphasis added).

81. Gilles Kepel, *The Revenge of God: The Resurgence of Islam, Christianity and Judaism in the Modern World* (Cambridge: Polity Press, 1994).

82. Jim Hoagland, "Facing Faith as Politics," the *Washington Post*, January 15, 2006, B07. For an examination of U.S. diplomacy's resistance to engaging religious actors and ideas, see Farr, *World of Faith and Freedom*, chaps. 1 and 2.

83. Farr, *World of Faith and Freedom*, chaps. 8 and 9.

84. Grim and Finke, *Price of Freedom Denied*, 160–201.

85. Liz Gooch, "In a Muslim State, Fear Sends Some Worship Underground," *International Herald Tribune*, January 28, 2011. Available at http://www.nytimes.com/2011/01/28/world/asia/28iht-malay28.html?_r=1&scp=1&sq=shiites%20malaysia&st=cse; last accessed on November 5, 2011.

86. Grim, "Is Promoting Religious Freedom Dangerous?" 9. Cf. Grim and Finke, *Price of Freedom Denied*, 194–200.

87. William Inboden, "Religious Freedom and American National Security," unpublished manuscript, 2.

88. Grim, "Is Promoting Religious Freedom Dangerous?" 10.

89. Monica Duffy Toft, "Getting Religion? The Puzzling Case of Islam and Civil War," *International Security* 31.4 (Spring 2007): 97–131.

90. The discussion of Russia here closely follows that in Toft, Philpott, and Shah, *God's Century*, 132–33 and 163–66.

91. Grim and Finke, *Price of Freedom Denied*, 103.

92. Samuel P. Huntington, *The Clash of Civilizations and the Remaking of World Order* (New York: Simon & Schuster, 1996), 70, 209–18.

93. See, for example, `Abdolkarim Soroush, Mahmoud Sadri, and Ahmad Sadri, *Reason, Freedom, and Democracy in Islam: Essential Writings of `Abdolkarim Soroush* (New York: Oxford University Press, 2000); Abdulaziz Abdulhussein Sachedina, *The Islamic Roots of Democratic Pluralism* (New York: Oxford University Press, 2001); Abdullahi Ahmed An-Na'im, *Islam and the Secular State: Negotiating the Future of Shari'a* (Cambridge, MA: Harvard University Press, 2008); Akyol, *Islam Without Extremes*; and Saeed and Saeed, *Freedom of Religion*.

94. Pew Forum on Religion & Public Life, "Rising Restrictions on Religion," August 9, 2011 (available at http://pewforum.org/Government/Rising-Restrictions-on-Religion.aspx; last accessed on November 5, 2011). See also the Pew Forum's earlier report: "Global Restrictions on Religion," December 17, 2009 (available at http://pewforum.org/Government/Global-Restrictions-on-Religion.aspx; last accessed on November 5, 2011).

95. Declaration on Religious Freedom (*Dignitatis Humanae*), on the Right of the Person and of Communities to Social and Civil Freedom in Matters Religious, Promulgated By His Holiness Pope Paul VI, on December 7, 1965. Available at http://www.vatican.va/archive/hist_councils/ii_vatican_council/documents/vat-ii_decl_19651207_dignitatis-humanae_en.html; last accessed on November 5, 2011.

96. John Courtney Murray, *We Hold These Truths: Catholic Reflections on the American Proposition* (New York: Sheed and Ward, 1960).

97. Brian Tierney, "Religious Rights: An Historical Perspective," in John Witte, Jr., and Johan D. van der Vyver, eds., *Religious Human Rights in Global Perspective: Religious Perspectives* (The Hague: M. Nijhoff Publishers, 1996), 17–45; Joseph Lecler, *The Two Sovereignties: A Study of the Relationship Between Church and State* (New York: Philosophical Library, 1952).

98. Akyol, *Islam Without Extremes*; Saeed and Saeed, *Freedom of Religion*.

99. Farr, *World of Faith and Freedom*, chap. 3; Fareed Zakaria, *The Future of Freedom: Liberal Democracy at Home and Abroad* (New York: W. W. Norton, 2003).

100. Grim and Finke, *Price of Freedom Denied*, 150.

101. Pippa Norris and Ronald Inglehart, *Sacred and Secular: Religion and Politics Worldwide* (New York: Cambridge University Press, 2004), 25.

102. *Johns v. Derby City Council*, February 28, 2011. Available at http://www.bailii.org/ew/cases/EWHC/Admin/2011/375.html; last accessed on December 2, 2011.

103. Michael W. McConnell, "Why Is Religious Liberty the 'First Freedom'?" *Cardozo Law Review* 21 (2000): 1265.